PowerPoint 2000 Made Simple

Moira Stephen

Routledge
Taylor & Francis Group

LONDON AND NEW YORK

First published 1999 by Made Simple Books

Published 2022 by Routledge
2 Park Square, Milton Park, Abingdon, Oxon OX14 4RN
605 Third Avenue, New York, NY 10017

Routledge is an imprint of the Taylor & Francis Group, an informa business

British Library Cataloguing in Publication Data
A catalogue record for this book is available from the British Library

ISBN 978-0-750-64177-7 (pbk)

Typeset by Elle and P. K. McBride, Southampton
Icons designed by Sarah Ward © 1994

Contents

Preface

Making a presentation is something that most people have to do at some time in their lives. It may be something that you do regularly or something that you are called upon to do infrequently – perhaps at a school or club meeting, or as part of a course you are studying.

A good presentation takes skill. Part of that skill is being able to create appropriate support materials – and this is where PowerPoint can help! PowerPoint can be used to produce all the materials that you need for your presentation – slides, overheads, handouts, speakers notes etc.

This book will introduce you to many PowerPoint features that can help you ensure that your presentation is a success.

Chapters 1–2 introduce PowerPoint and the Help system.

Chapters 3–5 cover the basic skills required to help you create and work with your slides.

Chapters 6–8 discuss some of the objects that can be used to add impact to your slides, e.g. WordArt, charts, tables, organisation charts, pictures and music.

In Chapter 9 you'll find out about the Master layout behind each slide/handout, etc. and see how you can use the master to promote a consistent look across your materials.

If you are going to give your presentation on a computer, Chapter 10 will give you lots of ideas, tips and tricks that will help contribute to its success.

Printing presentation materials is discussed in Chapter 11.

In Chapter 12 you will learn how to create hyperlinks to take you around your presentation, to other files, or to Web sites.

Don't be afraid to experiment with the features and you'll be creating informative, eye-catching presentations in no time!

1 Getting Started

What is PowerPoint?

PowerPoint is a presentation graphics package. If you have to make presentations, PowerPoint gives you the tools you need to produce your own materials with little or no help from presentation graphics specialists.

You can use PowerPoint to produce:

Slides

Slides are the individual pages of your presentation. They may contain text, graphs, clip art, tables, drawings, animation, video clips, visuals created in other applications, shapes – and more!! PowerPoint will allow you to run your slide show on your computer, or as 35mm slides or overhead projector transparencies.

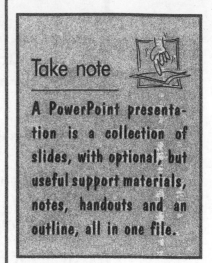

Take note

A PowerPoint presentation is a collection of slides, with optional, but useful support materials, notes, handouts and an outline, all in one file.

Speaker's notes (Chapters 9 and 11)

A speaker's notes page accompanies each slide you create. Each notes page contains a small image of the slide plus any notes you type in. You can print the pages and use them to prompt you during your presentation.

Handouts (Chapters 9 and 11)

Handouts consist of smaller, printed versions of your slides which can be printed 2, 3, 6 or 9 slides to a page. They provide useful backup material for your audience and can be customised with your company name or logo.

Outline (Chapters 4 and 11)

A presentation Outline contains the slide titles and main text items, but neither art nor text typed in using the text tool. The Outline gives a useful overview of your presentation's structure.

Basic steps

1 Click the Start button on the Taskbar.

2 Select Programs.

3 Choose PowerPoint.

Is PowerPoint installed on your computer? If it isn't, install it now (or get someone else to do it for you).

If necessary, switch on your computer and go into Windows. You are now ready to start.

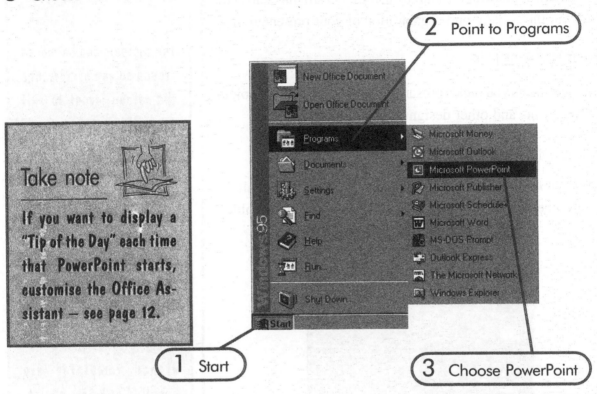

2 Point to Programs

1 Start

3 Choose PowerPoint

Take note

If you want to display a "Tip of the Day" each time that PowerPoint starts, customise the Office Assistant — see page 12.

Tip

If you have the Microsoft Office Shortcut Bar displayed, click 🔲 to start PowerPoint.

Take note

To leave PowerPoint just click on the Close button or open the File menu and choose Exit.

PowerPoint dialog box

You arrive at the PowerPoint dialog box, where you start to set up your presentation.

AutoContent wizard

Choose this if you want to start by using a wizard that helps you work out the content and organisation of your presentation.

Design Template

This option lets you pick a presentation template with the colour scheme, fonts and other design features already set up.

Blank presentation

If you opt for this one, you get a blank presentation with all the colour scheme, font and design features set to the default values.

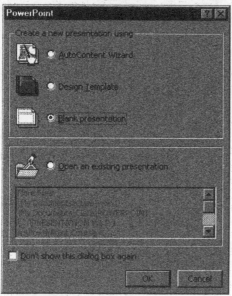

Open an existing presentation

This option takes you to the Open dialog box, where you can open an existing presentation.

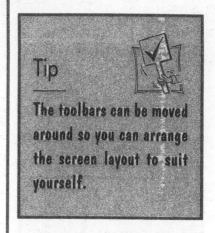

Tip

The toolbars can be moved around so you can arrange the screen layout to suit yourself.

Take note

Some professionally designed templates are supplied with PowerPoint. When you create a presentation by selecting the Design Template option a list of alternatives are displayed (see page 24).

PowerPoint window

Tip

Don't panic if your toolbars and menus are not exactly the same as those in this book – if you can't see a tool on the main bar, click the drop-down arrow at the far right to display more tools.

The PowerPoint window is very similar to other Microsoft application windows. If you use Word, Excel or Access you will recognise some of the tools on the toolbars.

The Standard and Formatting toolbars usually appear along the top of the window. The Drawing toolbar is usually along the bottom of the window.

Office 2000 applications personalise your menus and toolbars automatically, adding to them the items that you use most often. You can expand the menus to reveal all commands. After you select a command, it appears on your personalised menu.

The Standard and Formatting toolbars can share a single row on the screen, to leave more room for your work. When you click a button on a toolbar, that button is added to the personalised toolbars on your screen.

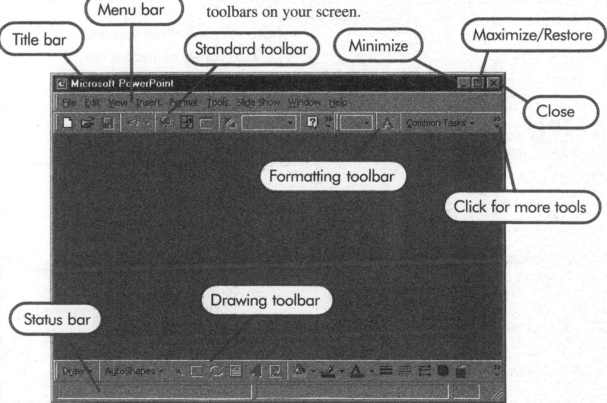

Menu bar

Title bar

Standard toolbar

Minimize

Maximize/Restore

Close

Formatting toolbar

Click for more tools

Drawing toolbar

Status bar

5

PowerPoint objects

When working in PowerPoint you work with *objects*. The objects may be:

- ❖ Text
- ❖ Drawings
- ❖ Graphs
- ❖ Organization charts
- ❖ Clip art
- ❖ Movies
- ❖ Sounds
- ❖ Tables.

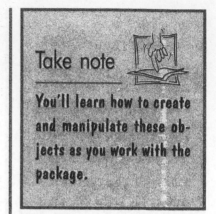

Take note

You'll learn how to create and manipulate these objects as you work with the package.

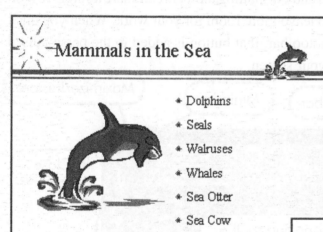

Mammals in the Sea

- ❖ Dolphins
- ❖ Seals
- ❖ Walruses
- ❖ Whales
- ❖ Sea Otter
- ❖ Sea Cow

Clip Art can enliven your text – a wide variety of images are supplied with PowerPoint

Annotated graphs can be produced very easily

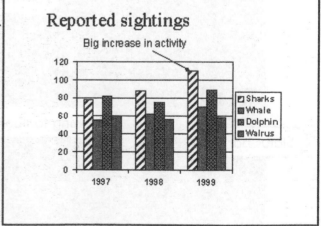

Reported sightings

Big increase in activity

Special text effects can be
created using Word Art

New Appointment Structure

Starts Spring 2000

R Adamson
Managing Director

M Dogsbody

C Stephen
Sales Director

P Anderson
Purchasing Director

K Stephen
Type title here

M Hames
Sales Rep

W Black
Sales Rep

R Peters
Ass'tant

P Milne
Chief Clerk

Organization charts are simple to
create – once you've worked out the
structure of your organisation!

Visitors to Education Centre

	Adult	Child	Member	Total
January	402	675	300	1377
February	542	865	430	1837
March	499	621	523	1643
April	1845	2300	1954	6099
Total	3288	4461	3207	10956

Tables are useful for
displaying statistics

Summary

- ❑ PowerPoint is a powerful presentation graphics package.

- ❑ The PowerPoint dialog box gives you a range of options to get you started creating your presentation.

- ❑ The PowerPoint window displays a selection of toolbars to give you quick access to commonly-used features in the package.

- ❑ To exit PowerPoint, click the Close button on the title bar.

- ❑ Text, drawings, graphs, Organization Charts, Clip Art, movies, sounds and tables are called PowerPoint Objects.

Tip

If you need to know more about Windows 98, try the companion volume in this series — *Windows 98 Made Simple.*

Take note

Not all of the features available in the application are installed automatically when Powerpoint 2000 or Office 2000 is set up on your computer. If you try to use a feature which has not been installed, a dialog box will appear on your screen. Follow the instructions to install the feature.

2 Help

Office Assistant

When working in the Windows environment there is always plenty of Help available – in books, in manuals, in magazines and on-line. The trick is being able to find the Help you need, when you need it. In this section, we look at the various ways you can interrogate the on-line Help when you discover you're in need of it.

The default route into the on-line Help is through the Office Assistant. This displays Help topics and tips to help you accomplish your tasks.

When you access the Help pages using the Office Assistant, the panel displays either a list of Help topics you may be interested in, or the Help page that you requested.

1 To display the Office Assistant press [F1].

or

Click the Office Assistant tool 🔲.

2 Click an item in the list for Help on that topic.

or

3 Type in your question and click ⌞Search⌟.

❑ A list of Help topic(s) will appear on your screen

4 Click on a topic to locate the Help you need.

5 To close the on-line Help, click 🗵 the Close button at the top right of its window.

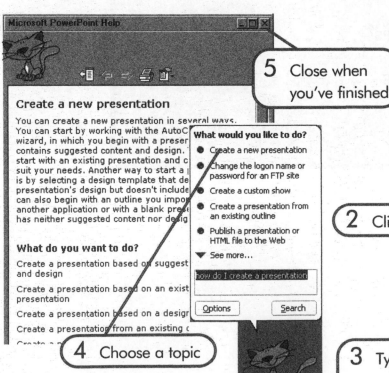

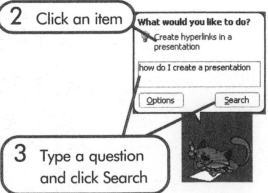

10

Basic steps

❑ To hide Office Assistant

1 Right-click on the Office Assistant.

2 Click Hide.

❑ To show it again

3 If you hide the Office Assistant, simply press [F1], or click ❓ to display it again when you need it.

or

4 Open the Help menu and select Show the Office Assistant.

You may keep the Office Assistant open while you work – you can drag it (by its title bar) to an area of the screen that doesn't obscure what you are working on, and leave it there.

To display its list of Help options (which vary depending on what you are doing), or to type in a question, simply give it a click!

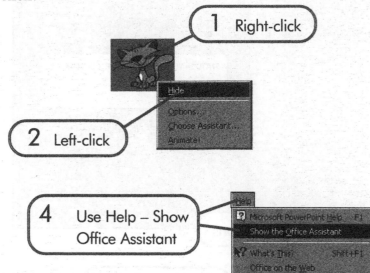

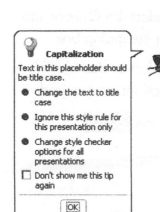

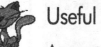

Useful tips

As you work in PowerPoint, you may notice that a light bulb 💡 appears on your screen from time to time. This is the Office Assistant telling you that it has a tip that you may find useful. Click the light bulb to read it.

11

Customising the Office Assistant

You can customise the Office Assistant to take on a different appearance or to behave in the way you find most useful.

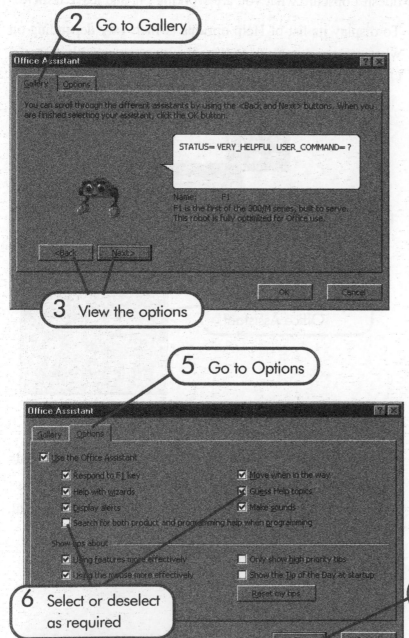

Basic steps

- ❏ To change the appearance of the Office Assistant

1 Click [Options] when the Office Assistant is displayed.

2 Select the Gallery tab in the dialog box.

3 Use Next> and <Back buttons to flivk through thr options available.

- ❏ To change other Office Asssistant options

4 Click [Options] when the Office Assistant is displayed.

5 Select the Options tab in the dialog box.

6 Select or deselect the options as required.

7 Click OK .

12

Basic steps

1 To open a folder, double-click on it or click its + sign.

2 Single-click to select a topic from the list.

3 The topic contain links to other Help pages – click on the links to reach the pages.

4 Work through until you find the Help you need.

5 Close the Help system when you're finished.

On-line Help

When you access Help with the Office Assistant switched off, the tabs that you can use to interrogate the system are displayed.

Contents tab

The Contents tab displays a list of the Help folders available. You may wish to browse through the folders to see what topics are included. Explore any that appeal to you.

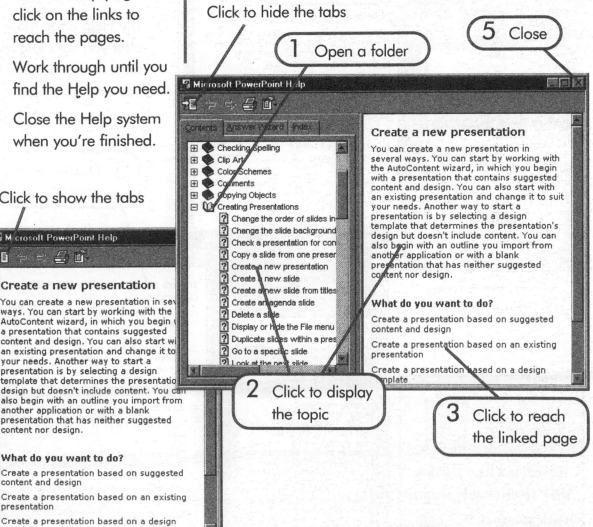

Click to hide the tabs

1 Open a folder

5 Close

Click to show the tabs

2 Click to display the topic

3 Click to reach the linked page

Answer Wizard

The Answer Wizard offers an alternative route into the on-line Help pages.

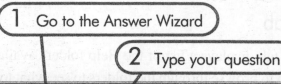

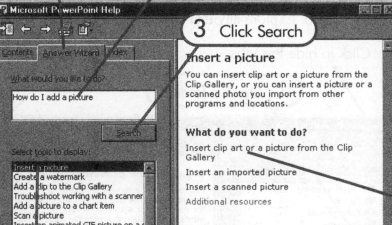

1 Select the Answer Wizard tab.

2 Tell PowerPoint what you want to do.

3 Click Search.

4 Select a topic from the list presented.

5 The Help page may offer you links to other pages – explore any that are of interest.

Take note

If you find a Help page you wish to print out, simply click the print tool 🖨.

Basic steps

1 Select the Index tab.

2 Type in the keyword(s) you're looking for.

or

3 Choose a keyword from the list.

4 Click Search.

5 Select a topic from the list in the lower pane. The Help page will be displayed.

6 Click the Clear button to delete the keywords if you want to perform another search.

Index tab

The Index tab gives you quick access to any topic and is particularly useful once you know what you are looking for!

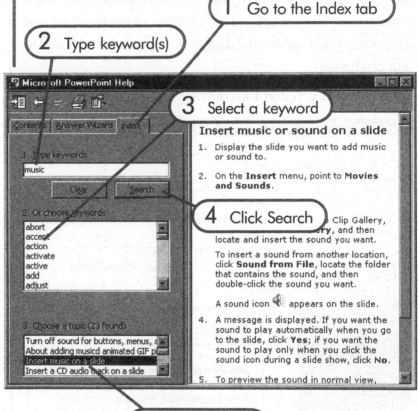

1 Go to the Index tab

2 Type keyword(s)

3 Select a keyword

4 Click Search

5 Select a topic

Tip

Use the Back ⬅ and Forward ➡ tools to move through the pages you have viewed.

Take note

If you have access to the Internet you will find more Help available there. Select *Office on the Web* from the Help menu.

What's This?

If you are new to Microsoft Office applications or to the Windows interface, there will be many things on your screen that puzzle you at first.

There may be strange looking tools on the toolbars; items listed in the menus may suggest things you've never heard of and other objects that appear and disappear as you work may add to your confusion!

Don't panic! If you don't know what it is – ask!

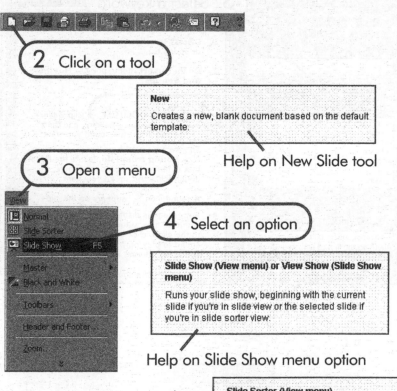

2 Click on a tool

New

Creates a new, blank document based on the default template.

Help on New Slide tool

3 Open a menu

4 Select an option

Slide Show (View menu) or View Show (Slide Show menu)

Runs your slide show, beginning with the current slide if you're in slide view or the selected slide if you're in slide sorter view.

Help on Slide Show menu option

Slide Sorter (View menu)

Displays miniature versions of all slides in a presentation, complete with text and graphics. In slide sorter view, you can reorder slides, add transitions and animation effects, and set the timings for electronic slide shows.

5 Click on any item

Help on Slide Sorter button

1 Hold down the [Shift] key and press [F1].

The question mark pointer 🔲 appears.

❑ To find out what a particular tool does

2 Click the tool.

❑ To find out about an item in a menu list

3 Open the menu list by clicking on the menu name.

4 Click on the option required on the menu.

❑ To find out about anything else within the application window

5 Just click on it!

6 Click anywhere on the screen or press [Esc] to close the explanation.

Basic steps

❑ To toggle the keyboard shortcut display

1 Open the Tools menu.

2 Choose Customize....

or

3 Right-click on any toolbar and choose Customize... from the shortcut menu.

4 Select the Options tab in the Customize dialog box.

5 Select/deselect the *Show shortcut keys in ScreenTips* option.

6 Click Close.

❑ Point to a tool on the toolbar – the keyboard shortcut will be displayed or hidden depending on what you did at step 5.

You can have large icons if you prefer

If you point to any tool on a displayed toolbar, a ScreenTip appears to describe the function of the tool.

If you like using keyboard shortcuts, you can customise the ScreenTips to display the shortcut as well. This will help you learn the shortcuts quickly.

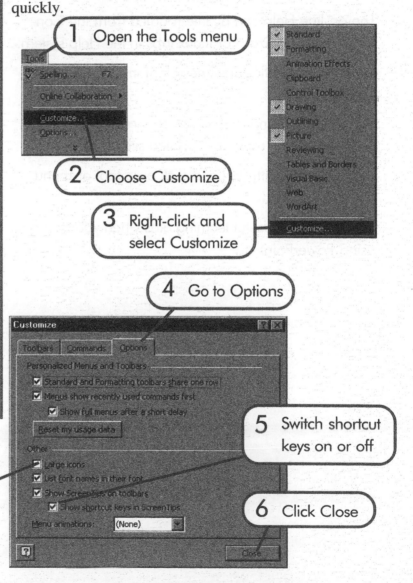

1 Open the Tools menu

2 Choose Customize

3 Right-click and select Customize

4 Go to Options

5 Switch shortcut keys on or off

6 Click Close

Summary

❏ Press [F1] or click the Office Assistant tool to get Help with your tasks.

❏ The appearance and behaviour of the Office Assistant can be modified.

❏ The Office Assistant can be hidden if you prefer.

❏ The on-line Help can be interrogated from the Contents, Answer Wizard or Index tabs in the Help system.

❏ Search for specific categories of information from the Index tab.

❏ If you have Internet access you can visit *Office on the Web* – a useful, regularly updated site.

❏ What's this? [Shift]-[F1] and click on a tool or menu item to find out.

❏ ScreenTips are useful learning aids when you start out using PowerPoint.

3 The new presentation

AutoContent Wizard

In this section we will look at the different options for creating a presentation – we will consider its content later. Whichever option you select, you still end up creating slides, notes and handouts for your presentation.

The easiest way to create your first presentation is to use the AutoContent Wizard. The wizard helps you set up the Title Slide (the first slide in your presentation), and gives you an outline to follow as you build up the other slides.

Basic steps

1 Start up PowerPoint and go to the PowerPoint dialog box.

2 Select the AutoContent Wizard in the PowerPoint dialog box.

3 Click ▭ OK ▭.

4 The first time you run this wizard the Office Assistant dashes to your aid! Close the Assistant if you wish and click ▭ Next > ▭.

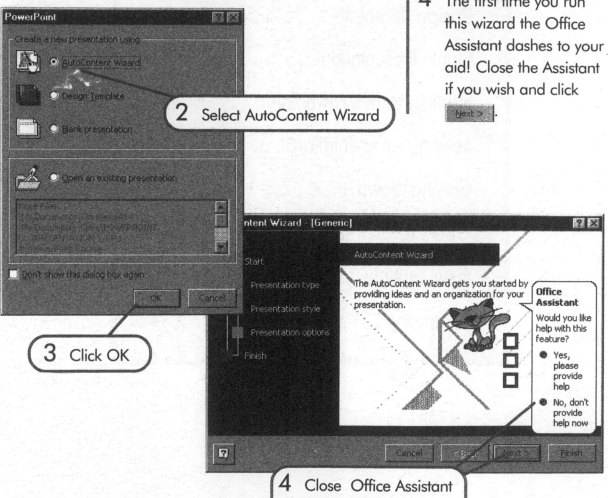

2 Select AutoContent Wizard

3 Click OK

4 Close Office Assistant and click Next

5 Pick the option that best describes the type of presentation you are going to give.

6 Select the presentation style – on-screen, Web, overheads or slides.

cont...

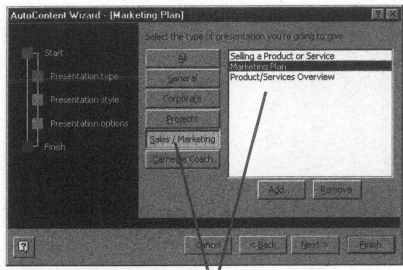

5 Select the presentation type

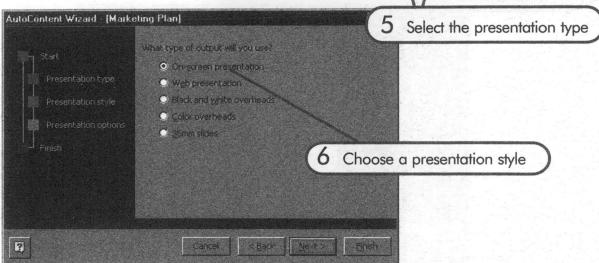

6 Choose a presentation style

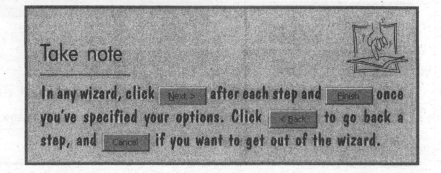

Take note

In any wizard, click Next > after each step and Finish once you've specified your options. Click < Back to go back a step, and Cancel if you want to get out of the wizard.

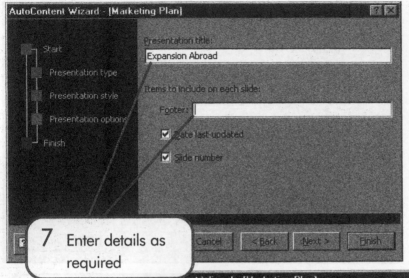

cont...

7 Enter the presentation title and any information that you want displayed in the slide footer area.

8 At the last screen click Finish. PowerPoint will set up your presentation.

7 Enter details as required

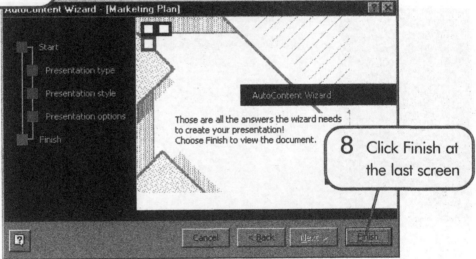

Those are all the answers the wizard needs to create your presentation! Choose Finish to view the document.

8 Click Finish at the last screen

Take note

Your presentation can be viewed on the screen using different views — Normal, Outline Slide, Slide Sorter or Slide Show. You'll soon learn which view is most appropriate to the task you are doing.

❑ Your presentation is displayed in Normal view.

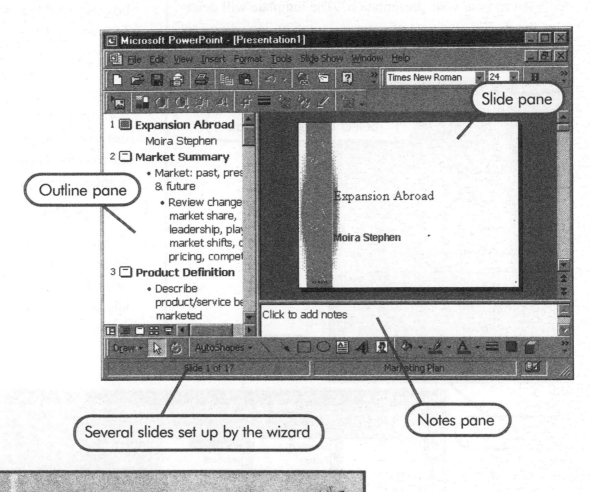

Outline pane

Slide pane

Several slides set up by the wizard

Notes pane

Take note

The AutoContent Wizard sets up several slides - the exact number depends on the choices you made as you worked through the Wizard.

Design Template

This option lets you start out by choosing the template on which you wish to base your presentation. The template will determine the design elements of your presentation, including font and colour scheme.

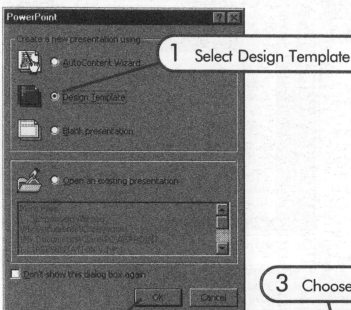

1 Select Design Template

2 Click OK

3 Choose a design

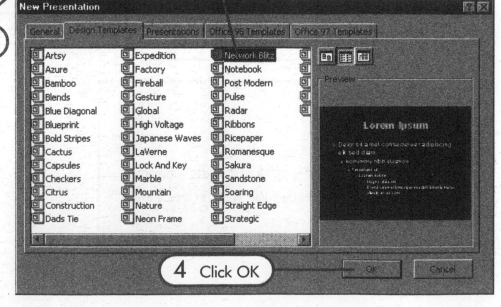

4 Click OK

1 At the PowerPoint dialog box select the Design Template option.

2 Click OK.

3 Choose the presentation design you wish to use from one of the tabs on the New Presentation dialog box.

4 Click OK.

❑ If you select from the Presentations tab, you are taken directly to the title slide of your presentation. Stop here!

❑ If you select from the Design Templates tab, you are taken to the New Slide dialog box to choose the layout for the first slide.

5 Select a layout.

6 Click ▢OK▢.

❑ Once PowerPoint has set up the presentation, it displays it in Normal view. The first slide is displayed, ready for your input.

Take note

If you don't like the look of your selected template, change it. Double-click on the Template name on the status bar. This takes you to the Apply Design Template dialog box where you can select a different template.

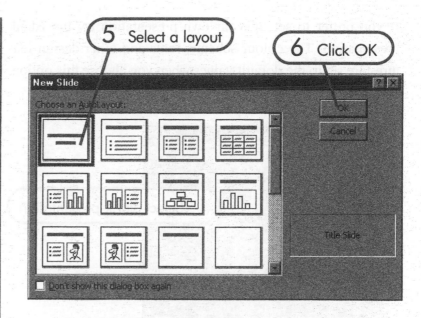

5 Select a layout

6 Click OK

Presentation in normal view

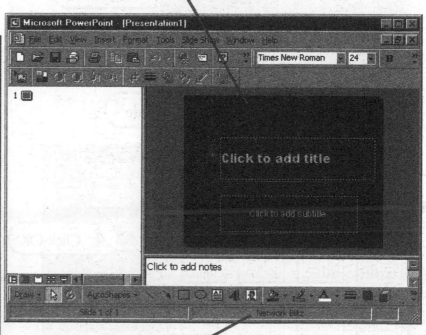

Template name

Blank Presentation

If you prefer to set up your own presentation try the Blank presentation. The colour scheme, fonts and other design features are set to the default values when you choose this option.

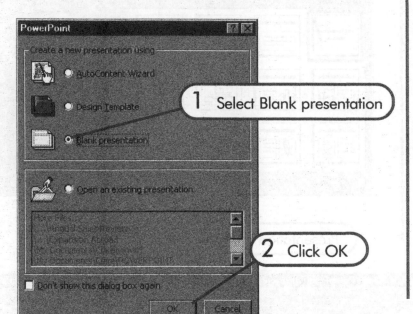

1 Select Blank presentation

2 Click OK

3 Pick the layout for the first slide

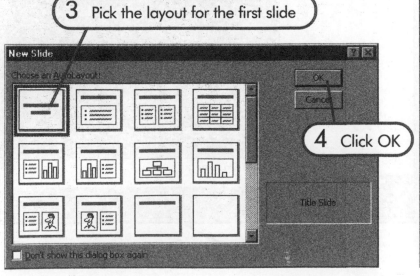

4 Click OK

1 At the PowerPoint dialog box select the Blank presentation option.

2 Click OK.

3 Choose a slide layout for your first slide – usually the title slide.

4 Click OK.

❏ Once PowerPoint has set up the presentation, it displays it in Normal view. The slide you chose at step 3 is displayed, ready for your input.

Take note

Some of the slide layouts in the New Slide dialog box have graphic, table, organization chart and clip art objects set up on them. We will look at these later in the book.

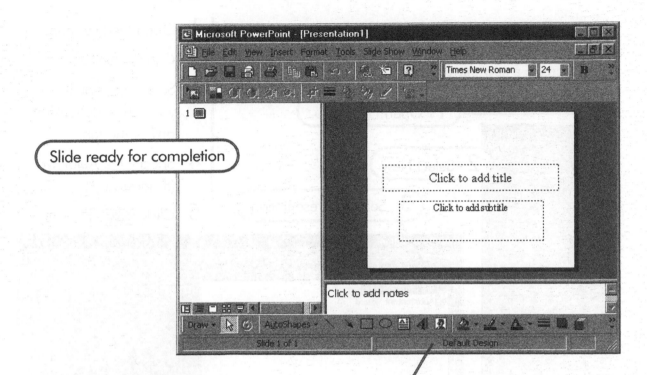

Slide ready for completion

Double click here to add a design template later, if wanted

Tip

If you don't like the structured approach of the AutoContent Wizard, you may find the 'clean' look created by the Blank presentation option easiest to work with in the early stages of setting up your presentation. The colours, templates and patterns can all be applied later.

Take note

The boxes with dotted outlines that appear when you create a new slide are called placeholders.

Different slide layouts have different placeholders set up on them — the placeholders will contain the slide title, slide text and any other objects you display on your slide.

27

Starting within PowerPoint

The PowerPoint dialog box is not the only place from which you can create a new presentation. When working in PowerPoint you can create a new one any time.

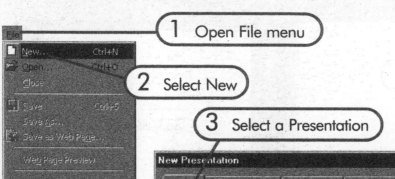

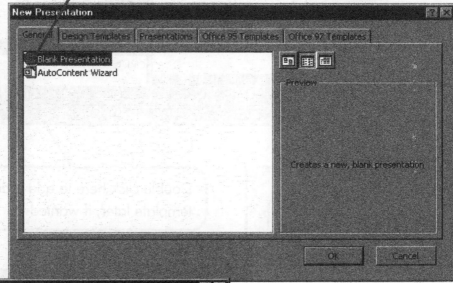

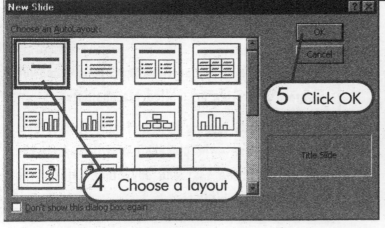

1 Open the File menu.

2 Choose New.

3 Select a template for your presentation from any of the tabs.

4 Specify the AutoLayout (if necessary).

5 Click OK.

Tip

To start with a blank presentation, click ☐ on the Standard toolbar. Select the layout for the first slide from the New Slide dialog box and click OK.

Basic steps

1 Click 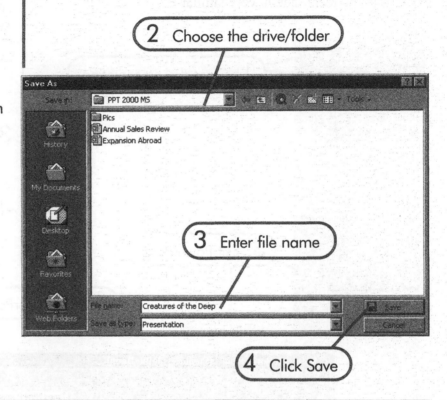 the Save tool on the Standard toolbar.

2 Specify the Drive and/ or Folder into which you wish to save your presentation.

3 Give your presentation a File name.

4 Click **Save**.

Saving a presentation

Once you have set up your presentation, you must save it if you want to keep it (if you don't save it, it will be lost when you close PowerPoint or switch off your computer).

2 Choose the drive/folder

3 Enter file name

4 Click Save

Save vs Save As

The first time you save a presentation, you are taken to the **Save As** dialog box to give it a name and specify the folder and drive you want it saved in. Thereafter, any time you save the presentation using the **Save** tool on the toolbar, the old version of the file is replaced by the new, edited version. This is what you would usually want to happen.

However, if you have saved your presentation, gone on to edit it, then wish to save the edited version using a different filename, or in a different location, open the **File** menu and choose **Save As** to get to the **Save As** dialog box.

Closing down

When you've finished working on your presentation you must save it (see previous page) and close it.

Leaving PowerPoint is very easy. If you use other Windows packages, the technique is very similar.

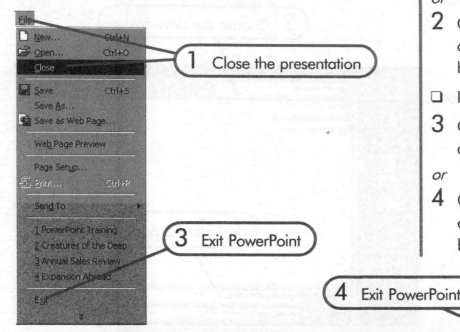

1 Close the presentation

3 Exit PowerPoint

4 Exit PowerPoint

❑ Closing a presentation

1 Open the File Menu and choose Close.

or

2 Click the Close button on the Presentation title bar.

❑ Leaving PowerPoint

3 Open the File Menu and choose Exit.

or

4 Click the Close button on the PowerPoint title bar.

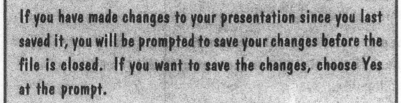

2 Close the presentation

Take note

If you have made changes to your presentation since you last saved it, you will be prompted to save your changes before the file is closed. If you want to save the changes, choose Yes at the prompt.

Opening a presentation

1 Click the Open tool 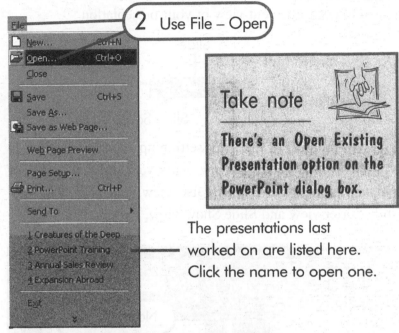 on the Standard toolbar.

or

2 Open the File menu and choose Open.

3 Select the Drive and Folder that contains your presentation file.

4 Select the presentation.

5 Double-click on the name or click [Open].

If you want to work on a presentation you've already created, saved and closed, you must open it first.

> 2 Use File – Open

File	
New...	Ctrl+N
Open...	Ctrl+O
Close	
Save	Ctrl+S
Save As...	
Save as Web Page...	
Web Page Preview	
Page Setup...	
Print...	Ctrl+P
Send To	▶
1 Creatures of the Deep	
2 PowerPoint Training	
3 Annual Sales Review	
4 Expansion Abroad	
Exit	

Take note

There's an Open Existing Presentation option on the PowerPoint dialog box.

The presentations last worked on are listed here. Click the name to open one.

> 4 Select the file

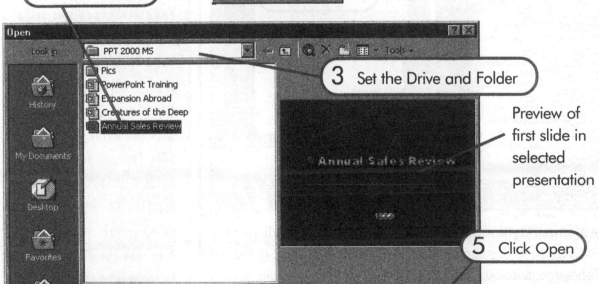

> 3 Set the Drive and Folder

Preview of first slide in selected presentation

> 5 Click Open

View Options

When working on a presentation, there are five view options. By default, PowerPoint displays all new presentations in Normal View. You can use the view icons at the bottom left of the screen to get a different view of your presentation.

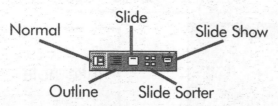

You will do most of the work setting up your presentation in Normal, Outline or Slide view – it's very much a matter of personal preference. You can also view your presentation in Slide Sorter view and Slide Show view.

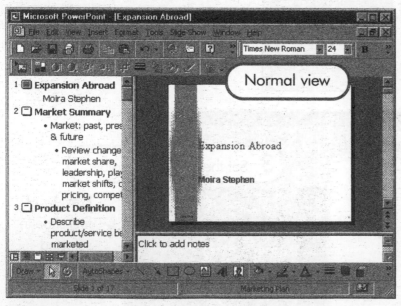

In Normal, Outline and Slide view, you have 3 panes displaying different parts of your presentation. The slide itself is in the top right pane, notes are displayed in the bottom right pane, and an outline of your presentation is displayed in the left pane.

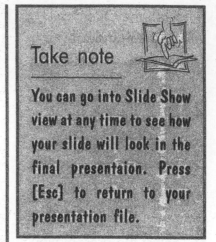

Take note

You can go into Slide Show view at any time to see how your slide will look in the final presentaion. Press [Esc] to return to your presentation file.

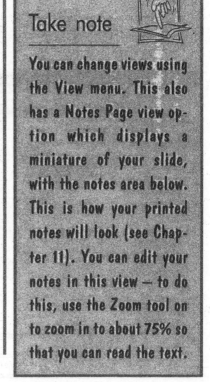

Take note

You can change views using the View menu. This also has a Notes Page view option which displays a miniature of your slide, with the notes area below. This is how your printed notes will look (see Chapter 11). You can edit your notes in this view – to do this, use the Zoom tool on to zoom in to about 75% so that you can read the text.

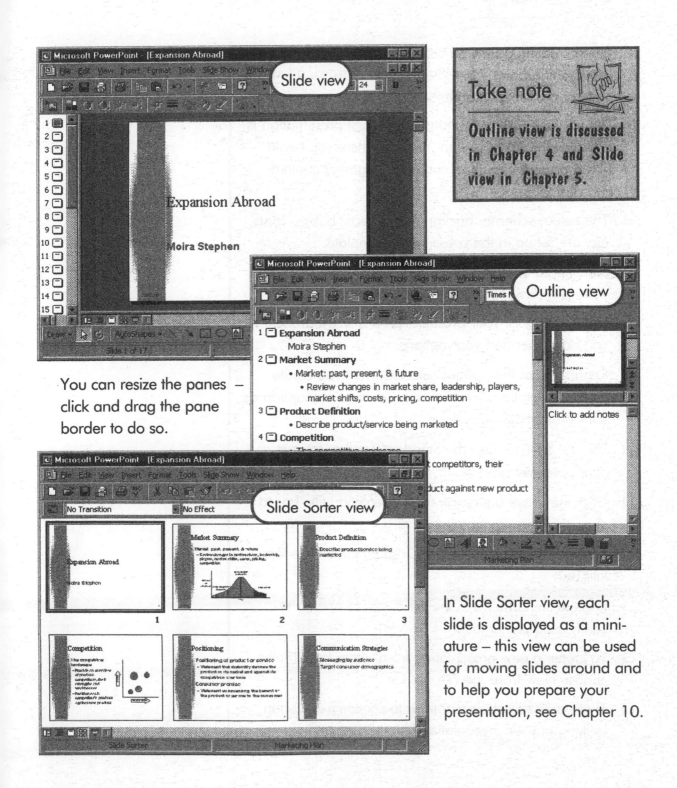

Take note

Outline view is discussed in Chapter 4 and Slide view in Chapter 5.

You can resize the panes — click and drag the pane border to do so.

In Slide Sorter view, each slide is displayed as a miniature — this view can be used for moving slides around and to help you prepare your presentation, see Chapter 10.

Summary

❑ When creating a new presentation, you can choose your starting point – the AutoContent Wizard, a template or a Blank presentation.

❑ The easiest/quickest option for your first presentation is probably the AutoContent Wizard, where you begin with a presentation that contains suggested content and design.

❑ The colour scheme, background objects, bullets, fonts, etc. are set up in the presentation template.

❑ Start with a Blank presentation if you prefer to set up your own design, or apply a template later.

❑ The first slide of your presentation is displayed once you have specified your options.

❑ Regardless of the options selected when you create your presentation, you can easily change any option as your presentation develops.

❑ Use the Save tool on the Standard Toolbar to save your presentation.

❑ Click the Close button on the presentation title bar to close the file.

❑ To Exit PowerPoint, click the Close button on the top title bar.

❑ Use the filename list in the File menu to open a recently used presentation.

❑ To create a new presentation from within PowerPoint, choose New from the File menu.

❑ There are several view options to choose from when looking at your presentation file.

4 Outline view

Setting up the outline

Once you've created your presentation, the next step is to decide on the text you want on your slides – the title and the main points to cover during your presentation. You can add text in either Outline view or Slide view.

In Outline view you can work on your text without the distraction of colour, graphics, etc. You can also determine the structure of the text on each slide (main points, subpoints, etc), using up to 5 levels if necessary.

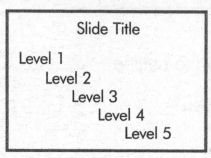

The Outlining Toolbar

You may find it useful to display the Outline toolbar when working on your outline. If it is not displayed, right-click on any toolbar that is displayed, and select the Outlining toolbar. It will normally appear down the left-hand side of the screen.

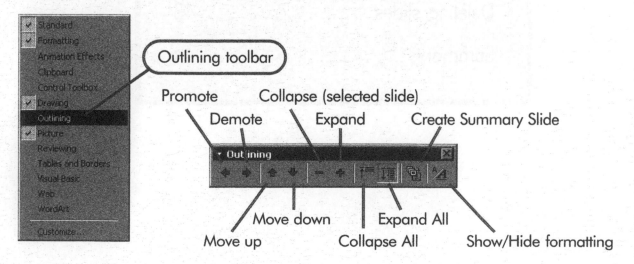

Basic steps

1 Go to Outline view.

2 Position the insertion point or select the text you want to replace.

3 Key in you own text.

4 Should you wish to make a list of points, simply press [Enter] after each point to move onto a new line.

If you used the AutoContent Wizard it will have set up a number of slides for you, with each given a Slide Title. Suggestions on the points you might want to make on each slide are also given. These should be replaced with your own points. (You can also change the Slide Title.)

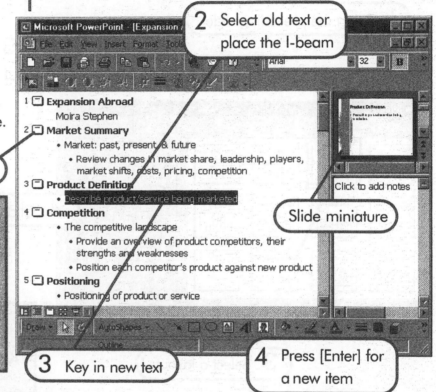

Slide icon

2 Select old text or place the I-beam

Slide miniature

3 Key in new text

4 Press [Enter] for a new item

Take note

If you opt to close the slide miniature, you can open it again from the View menu.

Selecting in Outline view

● **Click and Drag**

● **[Shift]-Click:** place the insertion point at one end of the text, move the I beam to the other end, hold down **[Shift]** and click the left mouse button.

● To select a point: single-click on the bullet to the left of the point (note special 4-pointed mouse pointer) or double-click to the right of the point.

● To select a whole slide: single-click on the slide icon to the left of the slide.

New slides

Regardless of how you create your presentation, you will need to add new slides at some stage. You can add new slides at any place in your presentation (not just at the end).

Try adding a new slide in Outline view.

(1) Select the preceding slide

(2) Click the New Slide Tool

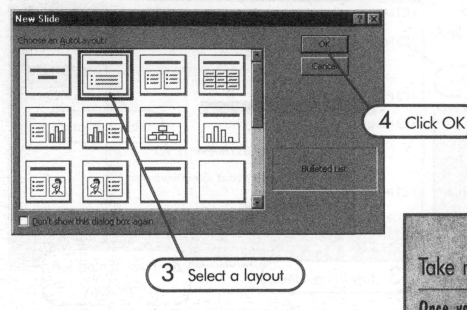

New Slide

Choose an AutoLayout:

OK

Cancel

Bulleted List

☐ Don't show this dialog box again

(4) Click OK

(3) Select a layout

Basic steps

1 Position the insertion point inside the slide that you want to be above your new one.

2 Click the New Slide tool.

3 Select a layout.

4 Click ▣ OK ▣.

Take note

Once you have keyed in the slide title, pressing [Enter] creates a new slide using the bulleted list layout. If you wish to list some points under the slide title, you must click Demote to move into the next level (page 40).

Tip

The keyboard shortcut [Ctrl]-[M] opens the New Slide dialog box.

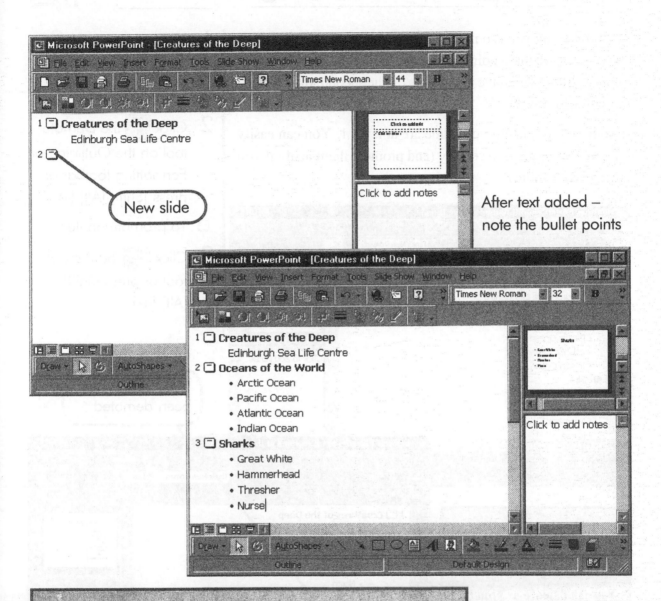

New slide

After text added –
note the bullet points

Promoting and demoting

The points you want to make on your slides will be structured – you will have main points (at the first bulleted level) and some of these points will have sub-points (at the second, third, fourth or even fifth level).

Initially, all points on your slide are at level 1. You can easily demote sub-items if necessary (and promote them again if you change your mind).

1 Place the insertion point in the item.

❑ To demote an item

2 Click ➡ the Demote tool on the Outlining or Formatting toolbar or press [Shift]-[Alt]-[→].

❑ To promote an item

3 Click ⬅ the Promote tool or press [Shift]-[Alt]-[←].

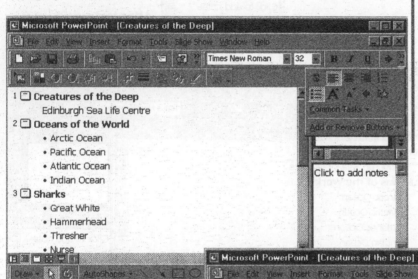

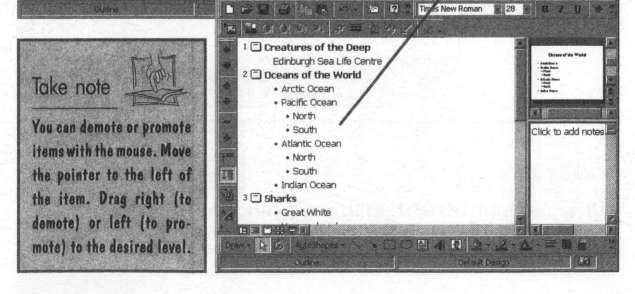

These items have been demoted

Take note

You can demote or promote items with the mouse. Move the pointer to the left of the item. Drag right (to demote) or left (to promote) to the desired level.

Basic steps

- ❏ Collapse selected slides

1 Select the set, or place the insertion point within a single slide.

2 Click ▬ Collapse.

- ❏ To expand again

3 Select the title(s).

4 Click ✦ Expand.

- ❏ All the slides

5 Click ▦ Collapse All.

6 To expand your presentation again, click ▦ Expand All.

If you want to get an overview of your presentation, or part of your presentation, you can collapse all (or part of) the outline down to show just the Slide Titles. The outline can then be expanded again to show the text as required.

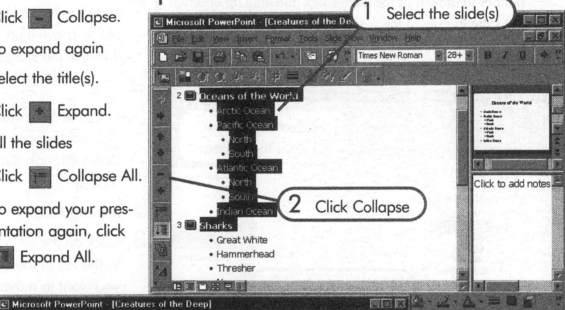

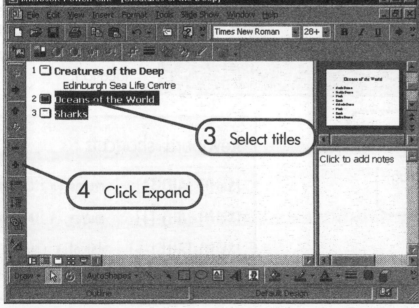

Rearranging an outline

If you decide that you want to change the order of the points you have made, this is very easily done in Outline view.

● If you prefer, you can also click and drag to rearrange points, rather than using the tools. Move the mouse pointer to the left of the item. Click and drag up or down until the item is in the required position.

❏ Moving items

1 Select, or place the insertion point in the item you wish to move.

2 Click the Move Up tool ⬆ to move it up through the slide(s).

or

Click the Move Down ⬇ tool to move it down through the slide(s).

❏ Moving slides

3 Click on the slide icon to the left of the one you want to move.

4 Use the tools, mouse or keyboard to move the whole slide to its new location.

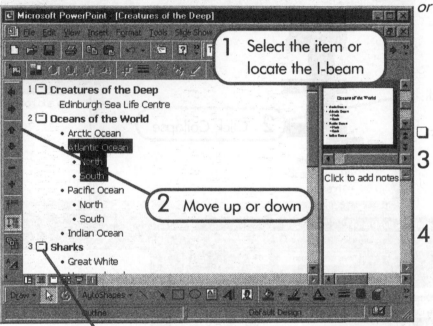

1 Select the item or locate the I-beam

2 Move up or down

3 Click on the icon

4 Use the tools or drag into new location

Keyboard shortcuts

[Shift]-[Alt]-[↑]	moves an item up
[Shift]-[Alt]-[↓]	moves an item down
[Shift]-[Alt]-[→]	demotes a point
[Shift]-[Alt]-[←]	promotes a point

Basic steps

1 Click the slide icon on the left of the title to select the slide.

2 Press [Delete].

If you need to remove a slide it can easily be deleted in Outline view.

Take note

You can delete slides in Outline view, Slide view, Normal view or Slide Sorter view.

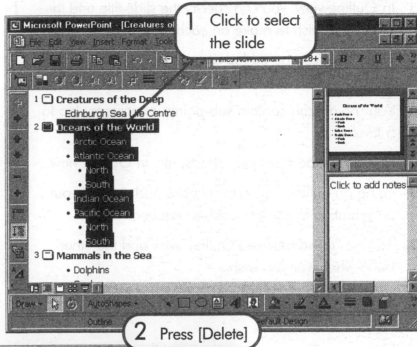

1 Click to select the slide

Microsoft PowerPoint - [Creatures o...]

File Edit View Insert Format Tools

Times New Roman | 28+ | B I U

1 Creatures of the Deep
  Edinburgh Sea Life Centre
2 Oceans of the World
  • Arctic Ocean
  • Atlantic Ocean
    • North
    • South
  • Indian Ocean
  • Pacific Ocean
    • North
    • South
3 Mammals in the Sea
  • Dolphins

Click to add notes

Draw ▾ AutoShapes ▾

Outline   Default Design

2 Press [Delete]

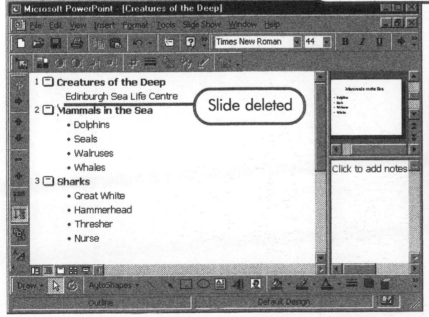

Microsoft PowerPoint - [Creatures of the Deep]

File Edit View Insert Format Tools Slide Show Window Help

Times New Roman | 44 | B I U

1 Creatures of the Deep
  Edinburgh Sea Life Centre
2 Mammals in the Sea
  • Dolphins
  • Seals
  • Walruses
  • Whales
3 Sharks
  • Great White
  • Hammerhead
  • Thresher
  • Nurse

Slide deleted

Click to add notes

Draw ▾ AutoShapes ▾

Outline   Default Design

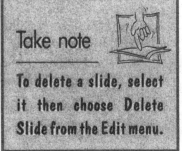

Take note

To delete a slide, select it then choose Delete Slide from the Edit menu.

Summary

- ❑ Outline view lets you concentrate on the text and structure of your presentation.

- ❑ In Outline view, you can specify the slide title and the points you wish to make on each slide.

- ❑ New slides can be added at any place in your presentation.

- ❑ Your points can contain sub-points if necessary (up to 5 levels).

- ❑ You cannot add pictures, charts, etc. in Outline view.

- ❑ Using an outline, you can collapse and expand your presentation to show the slides required.

- ❑ You can move between Outline view and the other views whenever you wish.

- ❑ You can rearrange the order or delete slides in Outline view.

5 Slide view

Normal view vs Slide view

The difference between normal, outline and slide view is simply the emphasis given to different parts of the presentation. If you wish to enter text directly onto your slide, you should go to either normal or slide view, where the slide pane takes up most of your screen.

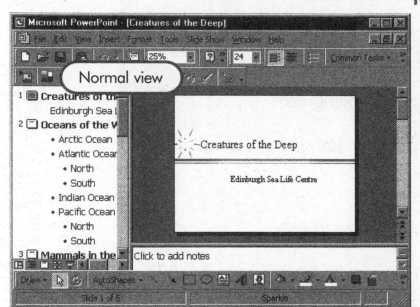

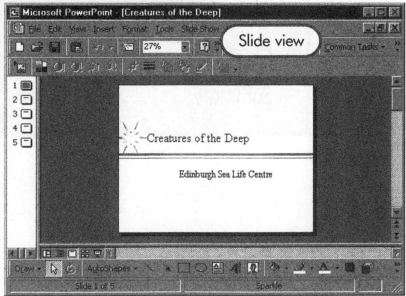

Basic steps

1 Drag the elevator up or down the scroll bar to display the desired slide.

❑ Note the slide number and presentation name that appears when you drag the elevator. When you let go of the mouse button, the slide appears on the screen.

or

2 Click the Previous Slide button to move up.

3 Click the Next Slide button to move down.

Moving between slides

In Slide view, you see one slide at a time on your screen. When you have several slides, you must move up or down through them to view them.

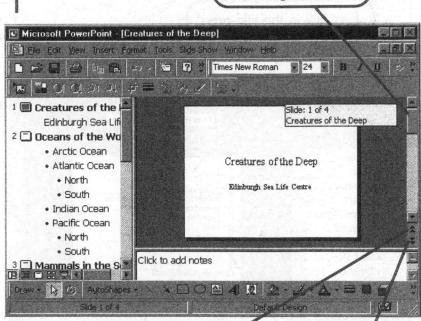

1 Drag the slider

2 Click Previous slide

3 Click Next slide

Take note

You can move from one view to another at any time.

Keyboard shortcuts

Press [Page Up] to move to the previous slide

[Page Down] to move to the next slide.

Entering and editing text

You can enter text in the slide pane in either Normal or Slide view (in Outline view the slide is a bit too small for working with text). To edit text on an existing slide, you must first locate the slide you wish to edit, then make the changes required.

❑ Adding text

1 Click in the title area.

2 Key in your text.

3 Click in the bulleted list area.

4 Key in your text and press [Enter] after each item.

5 Repeat step 4 until all your points are listed.

❑ Editing text

6 Click to place the insertion point inside the text to be edited.

7 Insert or delete characters as required.

An outline appears when you click in the placeholder

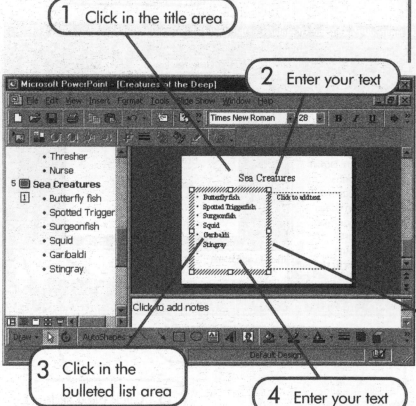

1 Click in the title area

2 Enter your text

3 Click in the bulleted list area

4 Enter your text

Take note

Use the Promote ◄ and Demote ► tools to structure the text on your slide.

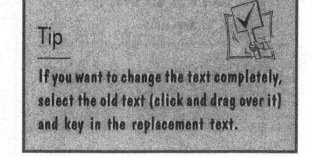

Tip

If you want to change the text completely, select the old text (click and drag over it) and key in the replacement text.

Basic steps

- ❏ To change the font name, size or style

1 Select the text you want to format.

2 Drop down the Font list and choose one.

or

3 Drop down the Font size list and choose one.

or

4 Click the Bold, Italic, Underline or Shadow tools to switch the format on and off.

5 Deselect the text.

So far, we've accepted the font formats attributed to our text by PowerPoint. You can of course change these at any time using the formatting toolbar.

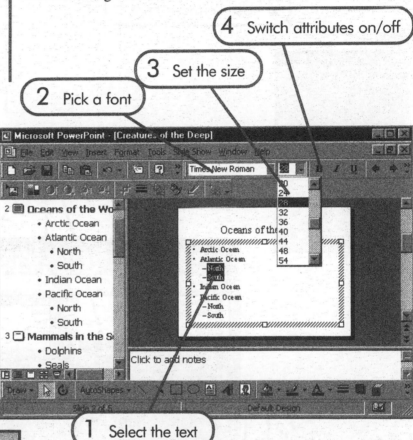

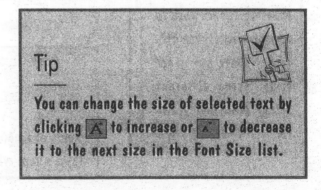

Keyboard shortcuts

[Ctrl]-[B]   Bold

[Ctrl]-[I]   Italic

[Ctrl]-[U]   Underline

These all toggle the style on and off

Tip

You can change the size of selected text by clicking Ａ to increase or Ａ to decrease it to the next size in the Font Size list.

You can also go to the Font dialog box to format the text on your slide.

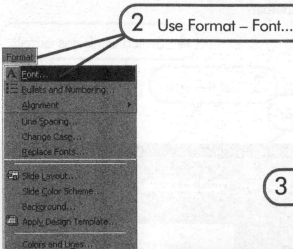

2 Use Format – Font...

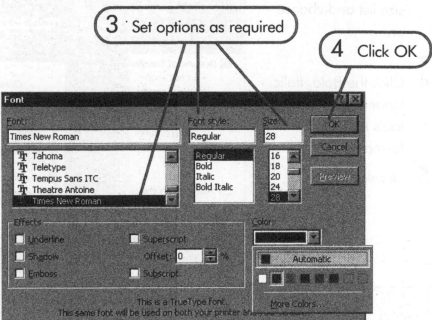

3 · Set options as required

4 Click OK

1 Select the text to be formatted.

2 Choose Font... from the Format menu.

3 Set the formatting options as required.

4 Click   OK   .

Tip

Most designers work to no more than three different fonts per page/ slide, using different sizes, bold and italic for extra variety.

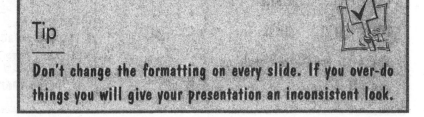

Tip

Don't change the formatting on every slide. If you over-do things you will give your presentation an inconsistent look.

50

Basic steps

1 Select the text you want to format.

2 Click the Left 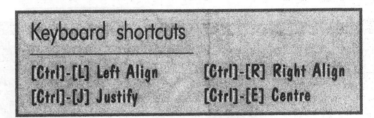, Center 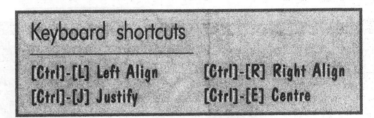 or Right 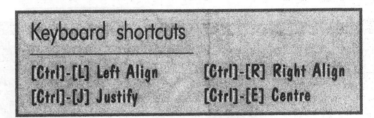 Alignment tool.

3 If you have selected multiple paragraphs or several characters, deselect the text.

Alignment

In presentations, text is usually aligned to the left or centre. There are tools for both of these and for right alignment on the Formatting toolbar. If you want text to be justified (making the text meet both left and right margins), there is an option on the Format – Alignment menu.

Keyboard shortcuts

[Ctrl]-[L] Left Align   [Ctrl]-[R] Right Align
[Ctrl]-[J] Justify   [Ctrl]-[E] Centre

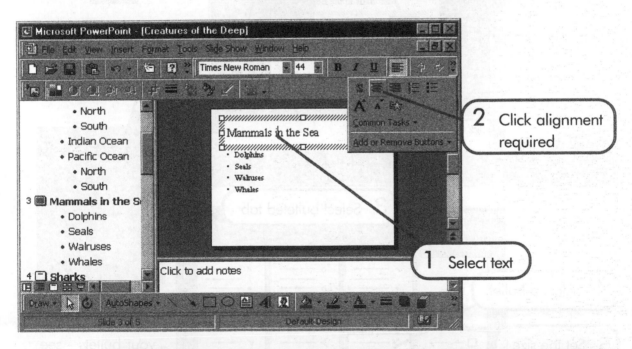

2 Click alignment required

1 Select text

Take note

A paragraph is selected if the insertion point is within it, or at least part of it is highlighted — you don't need to select all the characters.

Bullets

In most slide layouts the text objects are formatted to display bullets at each point. The bullets can be switched off (and on again) by clicking 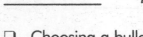.

● If you do not like the bullets set by PowerPoint, you can choose your own.

Basic steps

- ❏ Choosing a bullet
1 Select the point(s).
2 Open the Format menu and choose Bullets and Numbering.
3 Go to the Bulleted tab.
4 Select a bullet.
5 Set the colour and size.
6 Click ▭OK▭.

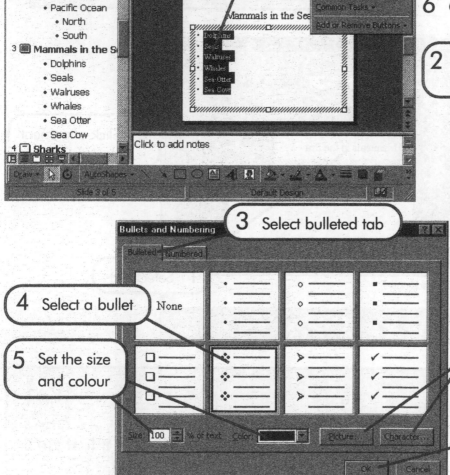

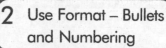

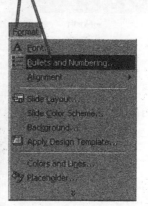

1 Select the text

2 Use Format – Bullets and Numbering

3 Select bulleted tab

4 Select a bullet

5 Set the size and colour

Click to customise your bullets – see the next two pages

6 Click OK

Basic steps

□ To select a different character

1 Work through steps 1-3 on page 50.

2 Click [Character...] on the Bulleted tab.

3 Select a character set in the Bullets from: field.

4 Set the Color and Size.

5 Choose a character.

6 Click [OK].

□ To edit a bullet

7 Work through steps 1-3

8 Edit the size and colour fields as necessary

9 Click OK.

Customised bullets

You can select from an even greater choice of bullets by going into the **Bullet** or **Picture** dialog boxes.

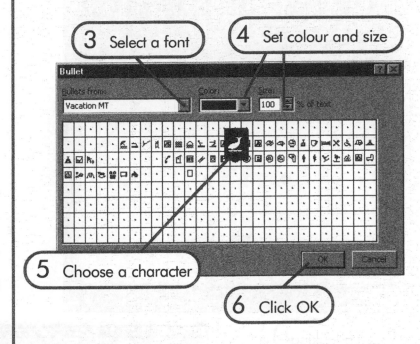

3 Select a font

4 Set colour and size

5 Choose a character

6 Click OK

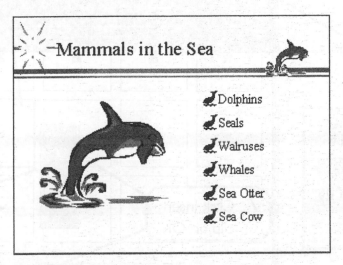

Picture characters often need enlarging to make their features visible

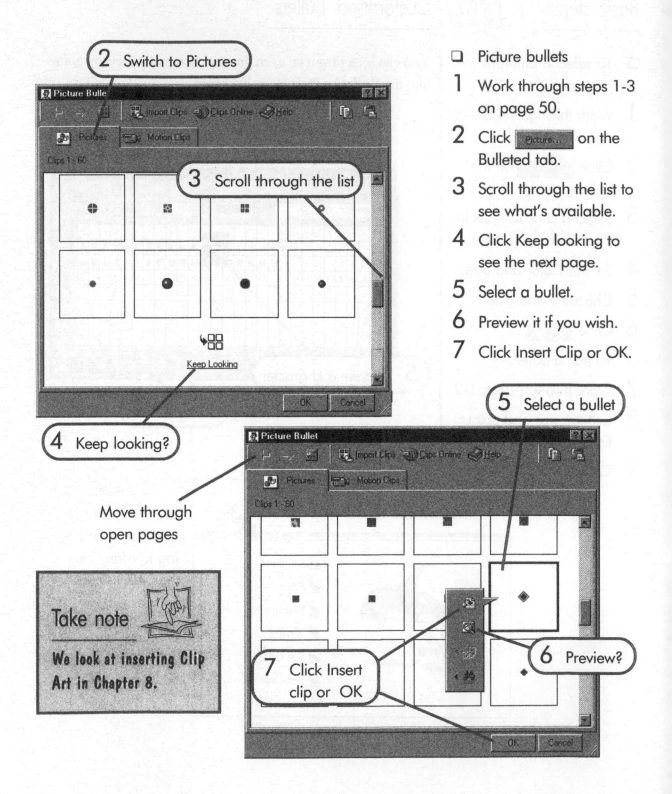

□ Picture bullets

1 Work through steps 1-3
 on page 50.

2 Click [Picture...] on the
 Bulleted tab.

3 Scroll through the list to
 see what's available.

4 Click Keep looking to
 see the next page.

5 Select a bullet.

6 Preview it if you wish.

7 Click Insert Clip or OK.

2 Switch to Pictures

3 Scroll through the list

4 Keep looking?

Move through
open pages

5 Select a bullet

6 Preview?

7 Click Insert
clip or OK

Take note

We look at inserting Clip
Art in Chapter 8.

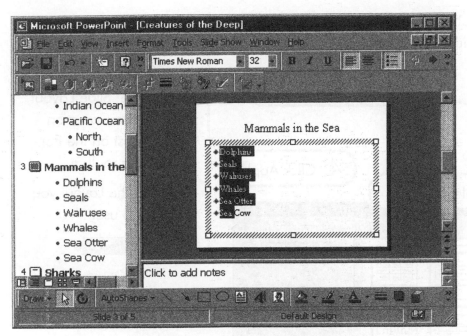

If you decide that you do not like the bullets, simply select the list again and repeat the steps to change them.

Lists can have standard or Roman numerals or letters – choose your style.

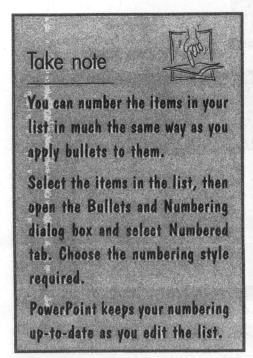
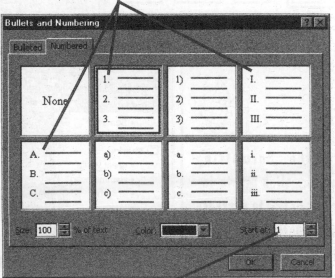

If you do not want to start the numbering at 1 set the start value here

Changing a slide layout

Basic steps

If you decide you have chosen the wrong layout for a slide, it is easily changed from Slide view.

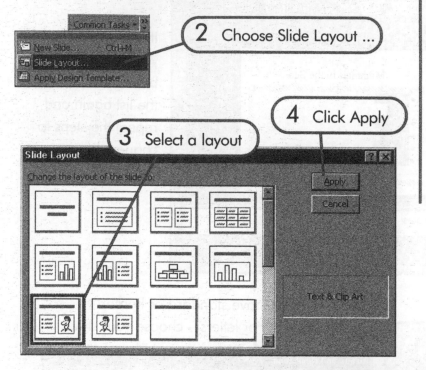

2 Choose Slide Layout ...

3 Select a layout

4 Click Apply

1 View the slide whose layout you wish to change.

2 Choose Slide Layout from the Common Tasks list on the Formatting toolbar.

3 Select the Layout you want to use.

4 Click Apply .

The new layout

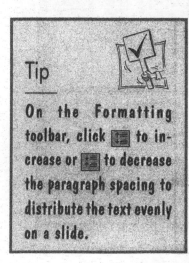

Tip

On the Formatting toolbar, click ▤ to increase or ▤ to decrease the paragraph spacing to distribute the text evenly on a slide.

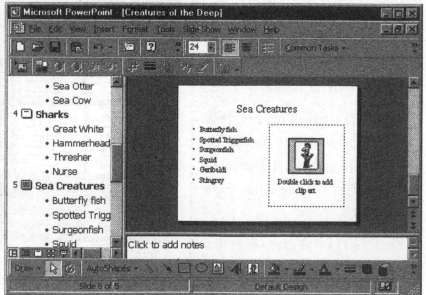

Basic steps

1. Double click the template name field on the Status bar.

or

2. Choose Apply Design Template from the Common Tasks list.

3. Select the template you want to use.

4. Click [Apply].

Changing the template

You can change your presentation template at any time. The template determines the design elements of your presentation - colour, fonts, alignment of text, etc.

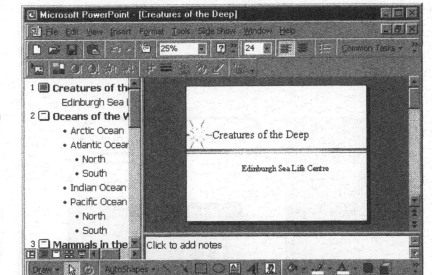

2 Choose Apply Design Template

1 Double-click the name

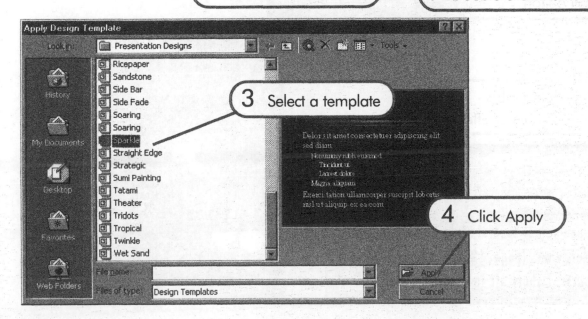

3 Select a template

4 Click Apply

Background styles

When you select a template for your presentation, the slide background colour and shading is picked up from the options set in the template. You can change the colour and shading options while retaining the other design elements.

If a presentation is in sections, e.g. on individual departments, or regional figures, you can set a different background colour for each section.

1 From the Format menu choose Background.

2 Select a Background Fill option from the list.

3 Click More Colours... and/or Fill Effects, if required, and select from the dialog boxes.

4 Click [Apply] to apply it to the selected slide.

or

[Preview] to see the effect.

[Apply to All] to apply it to all slides.

[Cancel] if you don't like the effect.

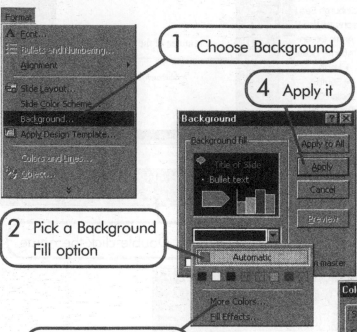

1 Choose Background

4 Apply it

2 Pick a Background Fill option

3 Select other colours or effects

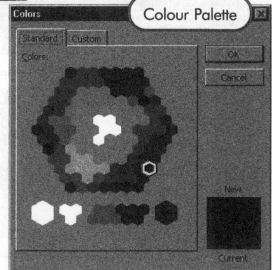

Colour Palette

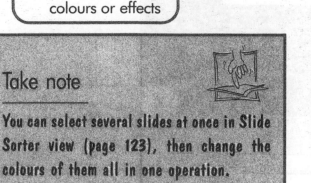

Take note

You can select several slides at once in Slide Sorter view (page 123), then change the colours of them all in one operation.

And yet more options.....

Experiment with the various dialog boxes to see what effects are available.

Specify your own shading
(1 or 2 colours) or choose
from the Preset Colours

Try one or the Textured fill effects

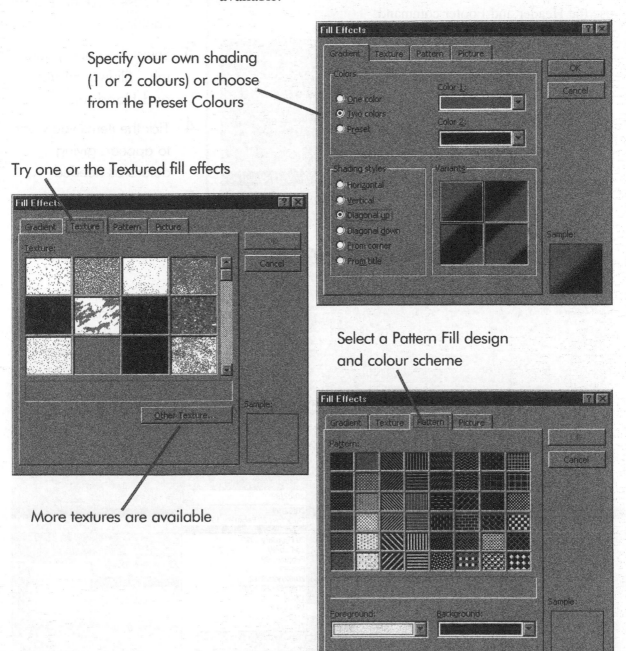

More textures are available

Select a Pattern Fill design
and colour scheme

Headers and footers

If you want to add slide numbers, the date, time or any other standard text at the top or bottom of slides, notes or handouts, use the Header and Footer command.

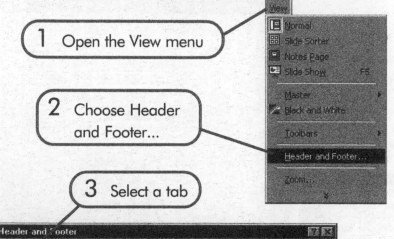

1 Open the View menu

2 Choose Header and Footer...

3 Select a tab

1 Open the View menu.

2 Choose Header and Footer...

3 Select the appropriate tab – Slide or Notes and Handouts.

4 Tick the items you want to appear, giving details as needed.

5 Click Apply or Apply to All .

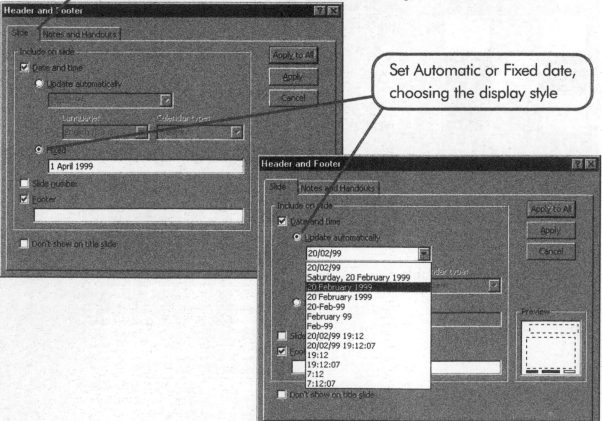

Set Automatic or Fixed date, choosing the display style

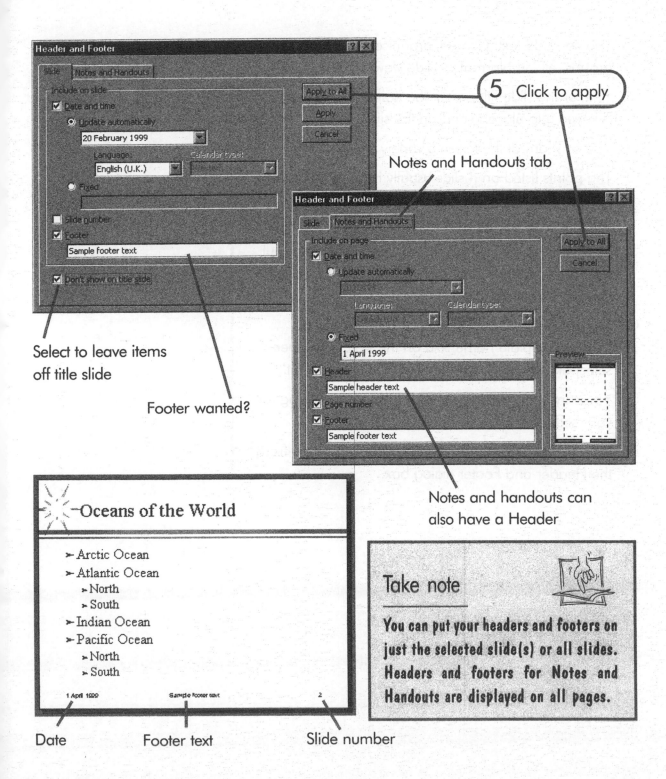

Header and Footer

Slide | Notes and Handouts

Include on slide

☑ Date and time
  ○ Update automatically
    20 February 1999
    Language: Calendar type:
    English (U.K.)
  ○ Fixed

☐ Slide number
☑ Footer
  Sample footer text

☑ Don't show on title slide

Apply to All
Apply
Cancel

⑤ Click to apply

Notes and Handouts tab

Header and Footer

Slide | Notes and Handouts

Include on page

☑ Date and time
  ○ Update automatically

    Language: Calendar type:

  ○ Fixed
    1 April 1999
☑ Header
  Sample header text
☑ Page number
☑ Footer
  Sample footer text

Apply to All
Cancel

Preview

Select to leave items
off title slide

Footer wanted?

Notes and handouts can
also have a Header

─☀─Oceans of the World

➤ Arctic Ocean
➤ Atlantic Ocean
  ➤ North
  ➤ South
➤ Indian Ocean
➤ Pacific Ocean
  ➤ North
  ➤ South

1 April 1999   Sample footer text   2

Date   Footer text   Slide number

Take note

You can put your headers and footers on just the selected slide(s) or all slides. Headers and footers for Notes and Handouts are displayed on all pages.

61

Summary

❑ You can add text, Clip Art, organisation charts, tables, graphs, etc. in Normal or Slide view.

❑ Text for the slide title, or for the points you wish to list, is keyed into placeholders on the slide.

❑ You can format the text in a variety of ways.

❑ The points listed on a slide usually have bullets beside them. You can switch these off, or choose a different bullet from the available character sets and pictures.

❑ To change the layout of a slide, click the Slide Layout from the Common Tasks list then choose the layout you want from the dialog box.

❑ To change the DesignTemplate, double-click the Design Template name field on the status bar, then select an alternative DesignTemplate from the list.

❑ You can easily change the background formatting for your slide.

❑ Headers and footers can be switched on and off from the Header and Footer dialog box.

6 Drawing and WordArt

Selecting objects

So far, we have dealt with text objects – slide headings and points listed for discussion on the slides.

In this section we are going to consider how the tools on the Drawing toolbar can be used to customise and add interest to your slides.

Select Objects tool

This is used to select objects on your slide. Once an object has been selected, you can then move it, resize it, delete it (and lots of other things as we'll soon see).

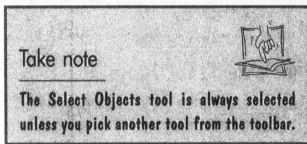

Take note

The Select Objects tool is always selected unless you pick another tool from the toolbar.

The Drawing toolbar

❑ To select a text object

1 Position the mouse pointer over any text within the placeholder area and click.

   Note the handles that appear at the corners and along the edges of the selected object.

❑ To select other objects

2 Click anywhere inside the object placeholder.

❑ To deselect an object

3 Click anywhere outside the selected object (click inside or outside a text object).

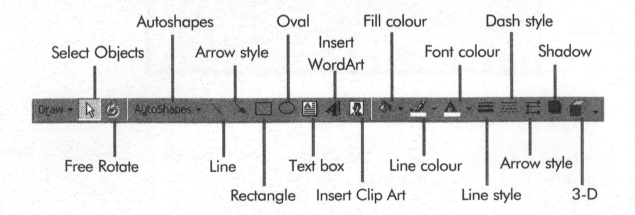

Select Objects — Autoshapes — Arrow style — Oval — Insert WordArt — Fill colour — Font colour — Dash style — Shadow

Free Rotate — Line — Rectangle — Text box — Insert Clip Art — Line colour — Line style — Arrow style — 3-D

❏ Moving

Point to the *border* of a text object, or anywhere *within* any other type of object (*not* a handle) and drag it to its new position.

❏ Resizing

Point to one of the handles (note the double-headed arrow pointer) and drag it until the object is the required size.

❏ Deleting a text object

Select the text object, click the border once, then press [Delete].

❏ Deleting other objects
Select, then press [Delete].

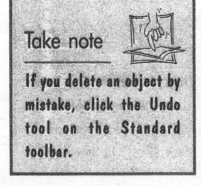

Take note

If you delete an object by mistake, click the Undo tool on the Standard toolbar.

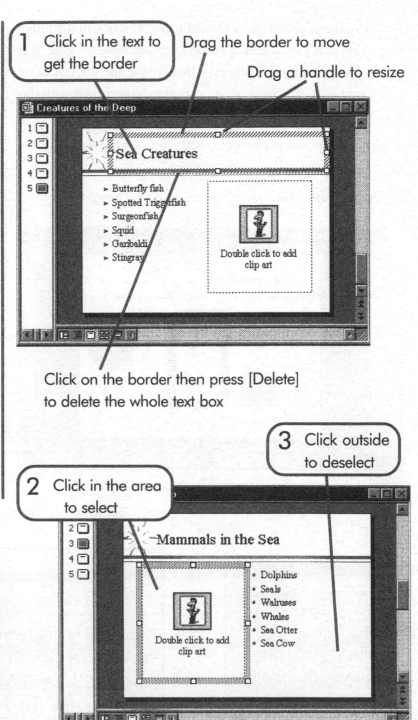

1 Click in the text to get the border

Drag the border to move

Drag a handle to resize

Click on the border then press [Delete] to delete the whole text box

2 Click in the area to select

3 Click outside to deselect

Drawing tools

The line, arrow, rectangle and oval tools all work in a similar way. You can customise a shape in many ways – give it a shadow, or 3-D effect, change the line colour and thickness, or experiment with fill colours and patterns. Experiment with the other tools to change the appearance of your objects.

If you need to position objects exactly, turn on the Ruler and/or Guides, using the View menu options.

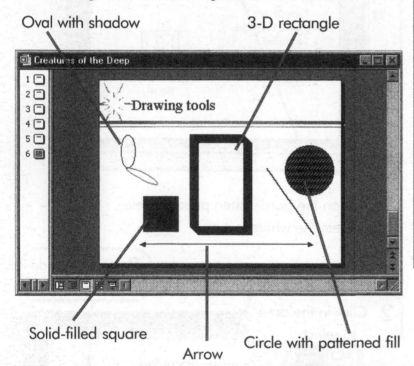

Oval with shadow

3-D rectangle

Solid-filled square

Arrow

Circle with patterned fill

❏ Line-based tools

1 Select a tool – line, arrow, rectangle or oval.

2 Click to set the start.

3 Drag to draw a shape.

❏ Different effects

4 Select the object.

Change the Fill or Line colour.

Set the line, dash or arrow style.

Add a shadow or 3-D effect.

5 Deselect the object.

Tip

To select a drawing object, click anywhere within it.

Take note

If you need to draw several lines, arrows, rectangles or ovals, you can 'lock' the desired tool on. Double-click a tool to lock it on. Draw as many shapes as you need. Select any other tool, or press [Esc], to unlock it.

Basic steps

1 Click the AutoShapes tool to display the categories available.

2 Select a category.

3 Choose a shape.

4 Click and drag to draw.

5 Drag the handle to adjust the shape.

❑ Freeform

6 Click and drag (note the 'pencil' pointer) to draw lines freehand.

Or, to get a straight line

7 Click at the start, then click again at the end.

❑ Curve

8 Click a path that you want the curve to follow.

9 Press [Esc] when done to switch the tool off.

You may find the shape you need under AutoShapes. If you want stars, triangles, arrows, etc. on your slide you'll find lots to choose from. AutoShapes can be drawn and formatted in the same way as the basic drawing shapes.

● The Freeform and Curve AutoShapes in the Lines category don't quite follow the basic 'click and drag' principle adopted by the other drawing tools.

Experiment with the various options.

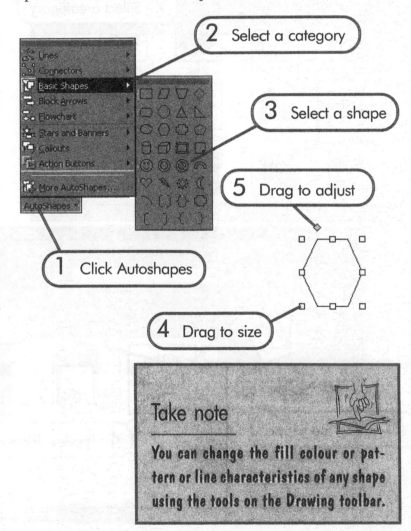

Take note

The Action Buttons are discussed in Chapter 12.

Take note

You can change the fill colour or pattern or line characteristics of any shape using the tools on the Drawing toolbar.

More AutoShapes

If you have used earlier versions of PowerPoint, you will find that there are even more AutoShapes to choose from in PowerPoint 2000.

You can search for clips by typing keywords

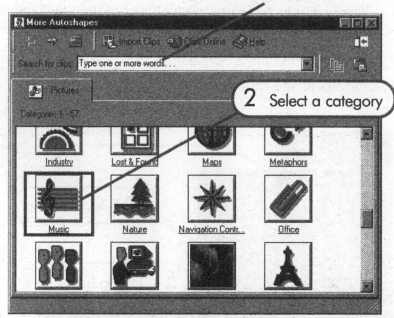

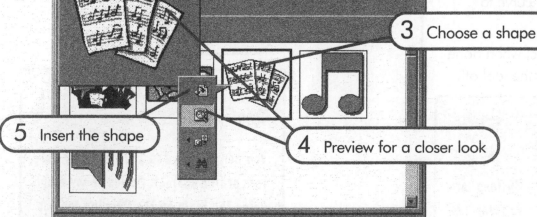

Basic steps

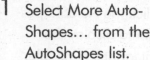

1 Select More Auto-Shapes... from the AutoShapes list.

2 Select a category from the More Autoshapes dialog box.

3 At the next panel, choose a shape.

4 Preview it if you want a closer look.

5 Insert the shape.

Take note

The tools for manipulating shapes appear automatically when you click on a shape.

Basic steps

1 Select the object that you wish to rotate or flip.

2 Choose Rotate or Flip from the Draw menu.

3 Select the option required from the submenu.

4 With the Free Rotate tool, drag a rotate handle to turn the shape the way you want.

Once an object has been drawn, you can flip it over horizontally or vertically, or rotate it right or left to get the effect you want.

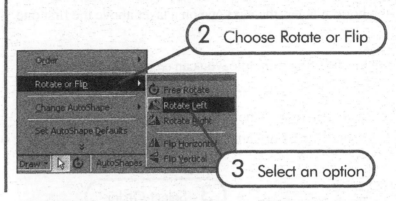

2 Choose Rotate or Flip

3 Select an option

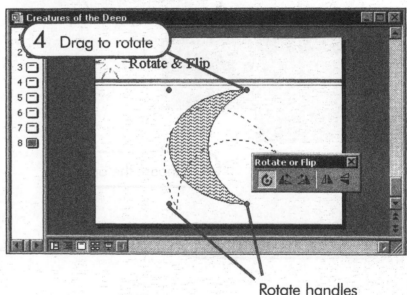

4 Drag to rotate

Rotate handles

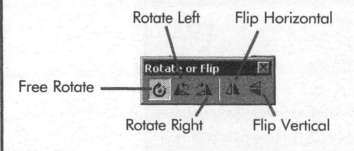

Free Rotate

Rotate Left

Rotate Right

Flip Horizontal

Flip Vertical

Take note

The Rotate or Flip submenu can be dragged to 'float' on your screen. Click and drag its title bar. Any submenu with a title bar can become a floating toolbar.

69

Changing the order

When you draw objects onto your slides, they lie in layers relative to the order in which they are drawn. The first object is on the bottom layer, the next one on a layer above the first one and so on.

Using this layering principle, you can create complex drawings by overlapping objects one on top of another.

If you need to rearrange the layering of your objects, you can do so using the Bring Forward and Send Backward commands.

Basic steps

1 Select the object you wish to Bring Forward or Send Backward.

2 Open the Draw menu.

3 Select Order.

4 Choose the option required.

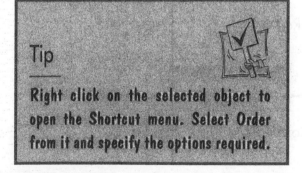

3 Select Order

4 Choose the option

2 Open the Draw menu

Take note

Bring to Front and Send to Back move the selected object to the top or bottom of the pile of objects. Bring Forward and Send Backward move the selected object through the pile one layer at a time.

Tip

Right click on the selected object to open the Shortcut menu. Select Order from it and specify the options required.

Basic steps

Group and ungroup

1 Select the objects you want to group.

❏ Select the first object then hold [Shift] down when you select the other objects.

❏ To select all the objects on a slide use [Ctrl]-[A] or drag over them.

2 Open the Draw menu.

3 Select Group.

If you have drawn several objects to generate an image, you can group the objects together into one to make it easier to move, copy or resize the whole image.

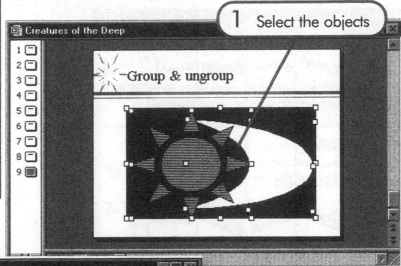

1 Select the objects

Grouped into one object

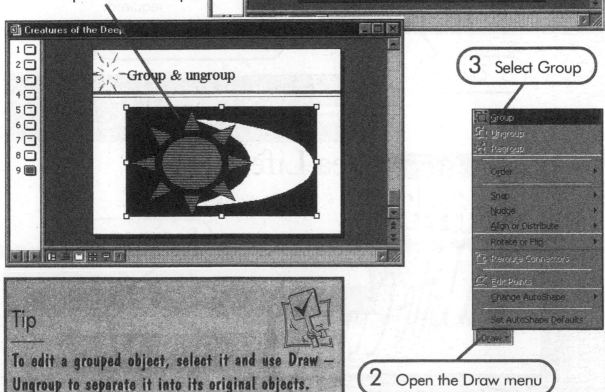

3 Select Group

2 Open the Draw menu

Tip

To edit a grouped object, select it and use Draw – Ungroup to separate it into its original objects.

WordArt

With WordArt you can create special text effects on your slides. It allows you to produce stunning title slides and real eye-catchers wherever they are needed.

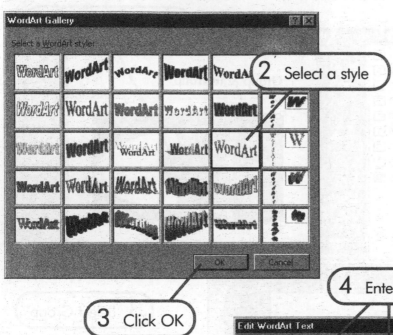

2 Select a style

3 Click OK

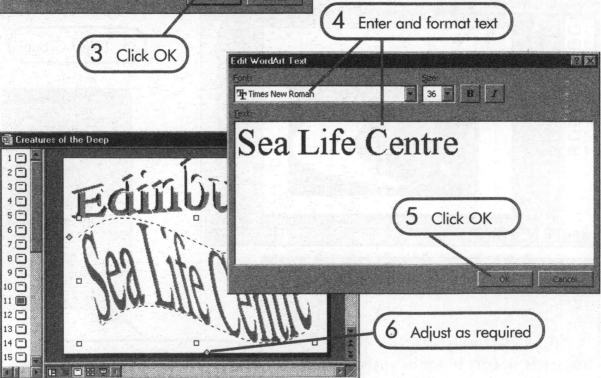

4 Enter and format text

5 Click OK

6 Adjust as required

Basic steps

1 Click the Insert WordArt tool ⬛ on the Drawing toolbar.

2 Select a WordArt style from the Gallery.

3 Click ⬛ OK ⬛.

4 At the Edit WordArt Text dialog box, enter (and format) the text.

5 Click ⬛ OK ⬛.

6 Adjust the shape of your WordArt object as required.

The WordArt toolbar

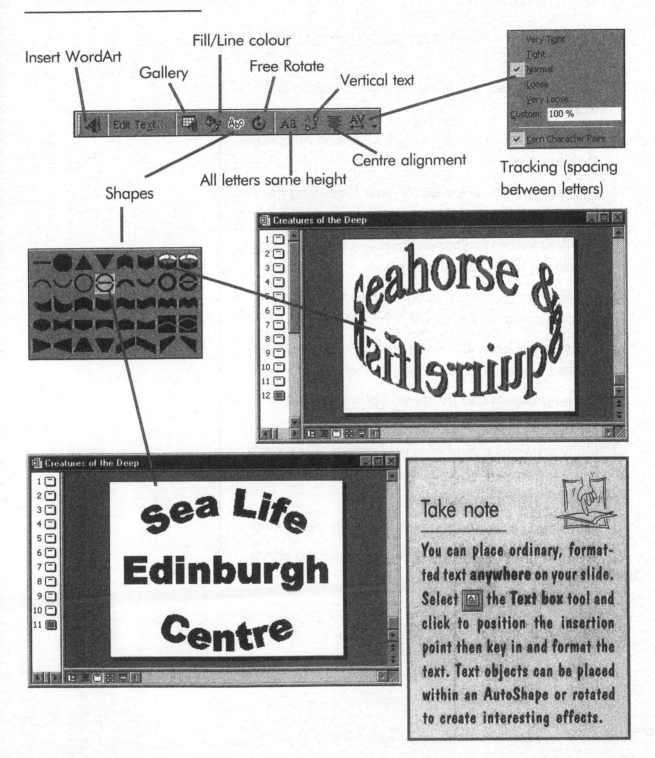

Insert WordArt

Gallery

Fill/Line colour

Free Rotate

Vertical text

Centre alignment

All letters same height

Shapes

Tracking (spacing between letters)

Very Tight
Tight
✓ Normal
Loose
Very Loose
Custom: 100 %

✓ Kern Character Pairs

Edit Text...

Take note

You can place ordinary, formatted text anywhere on your slide. Select the Text box tool and click to position the insertion point then key in and format the text. Text objects can be placed within an AutoShape or rotated to create interesting effects.

Creatures of the Deep

seahorse & squirrelfish

Sea Life Edinburgh Centre

Summary

- ❑ To move, resize or delete an object, you must select it first.

- ❑ A selected object can easily be moved, resized or deleted.

- ❑ You can use the Line, Rectangle, Oval and AutoShape tools to create drawings on your slides.

- ❑ You can add text anywhere on your slide using the Text box tool.

- ❑ The AutoShapes toolbar contains several useful shapes to add impact to your presentations.

- ❑ Objects can be rotated using the Free Rotate and Rotate tools, or mirrored with the Flip tools.

- ❑ Drawing objects can overlap each other and can be layered to produce the image you require.

- ❑ Drawing objects can be moved backwards and forwards relative to each other.

- ❑ Many drawings consist of several objects. The objects can be 'grouped' together to make it easier to move, resize or delete an image.

- ❑ Fill colours, lines and shadows are easily customised.

- ❑ WordArt gives you access to many special text effects.

7 Charts

Creating a chart

There will be times when pictures talk louder than words – and when this is the case you can use charts, organisation charts, clip art, tables, etc to help you make your point. In this section we'll look at ways you can add a chart or graph to your slide.

There are three main ways to set up your chart using Microsoft Graph 2000:

- choose a slide from the New Slide dialog box that has a chart placeholder already on it;

  or

- choose a slide from the New Slide dialog box that has an object placeholder already on it;

  or

- click the Insert Chart tool.

❑ Using a chart placeholder

1 Double-click within the chart placeholder to start Microsoft Graph.

❑ From a slide with no placeholder set

2 Click ▥ the Insert Chart tool on the Standard toolbar.

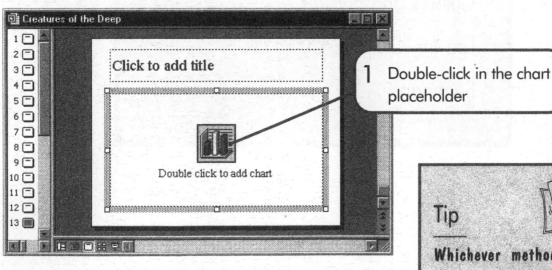

1 Double-click in the chart placeholder

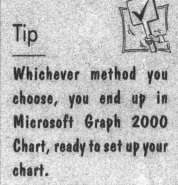

Tip

Whichever method you choose, you end up in Microsoft Graph 2000 Chart, ready to set up your chart.

Basic steps

- ❑ Using an object placeholder

1 Double-click within the object placeholder on your slide to open the Insert Object dialog box.

2 Choose Microsoft Graph 2000 Chart.

3 Click [OK].

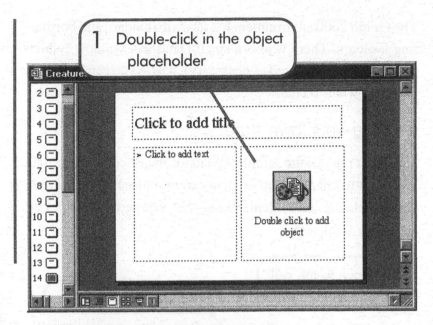

Double-click in the object placeholder

Click to add title

> Click to add text

Double click to add object

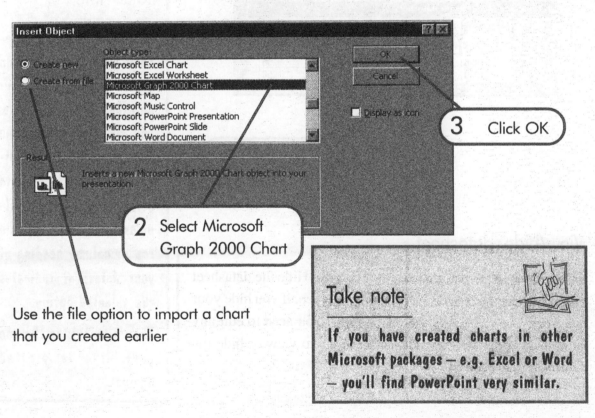

Insert Object

Object type:

- Create new
- Create from file

Microsoft Excel Chart
Microsoft Excel Worksheet
Microsoft Graph 2000 Chart
Microsoft Map
Microsoft Music Control
Microsoft PowerPoint Presentation
Microsoft PowerPoint Slide
Microsoft Word Document

OK
Cancel

Display as Icon

Result

Inserts a new Microsoft Graph 2000 Chart object into your presentation.

3 Click OK

2 Select Microsoft Graph 2000 Chart

Use the file option to import a chart that you created earlier

Take note

If you have created charts in other Microsoft packages – e.g. Excel or Word – you'll find PowerPoint very similar.

Datasheet and toolbars

The Graph 2000 environment has its own Standard and Formatting toolbars. There is also a small Datasheet window (which can be moved or resized as necessary), where you can key in the data you want to chart.

Entering your own data

You must replace the sample data in the datasheet with the data you want to chart. If you do not need to replace all the sample data, delete the cell contents that are not required – go to the cell and press [Delete].

1 Go to the cell into which you wish to enter your own data.

2 Key in the data.

3 Move to the next cell you want to work on, use any of the methods shown opposite.

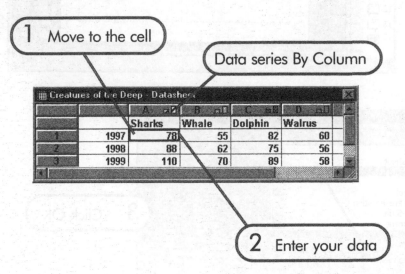

1 Move to the cell

Data series By Column

2 Enter your data

View/hide datasheet

Once you have keyed in your data, you can Hide the datasheet so you can see the chart clearly on your screen. If you hide your datasheet, you can easily view it again if you need to edit any data. Click , the View Datasheet tool, to view or hide the Datasheet, as required.

Take note

The Category axis has labels taken from the column or row headings in your datasheet. Use **By Row** and **By Column** on the Standard toolbar to indicate whether your data series is in rows or columns. A graphic in the row or column heading of your datasheet indicates the selected option.

The Value axis is the one your data is plotted against.

Moving around your datasheet

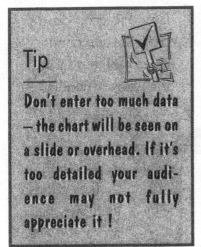

Tip

Don't enter too much data — the chart will be seen on a slide or overhead. If it's too detailed your audience may not fully appreciate it !

There are a number of ways to move from cell to cell within the Datasheet. Use the keys:

Arrow keys	one cell in direction of arrow
[Tab]	forward to the next cell
[Shift]-[Tab]	back to the previous cell
[Enter]	down to the next cell in a column

or

Point to the cell and click.

The cell you are in (your *current* cell) has a dark border.

Standard toolbar

Formatting toolbar

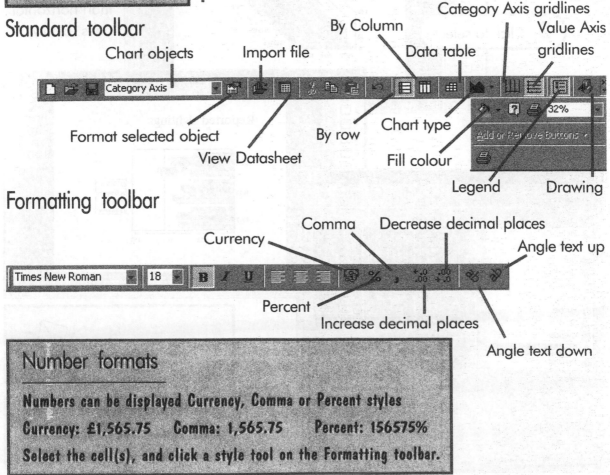

Number formats

Numbers can be displayed Currency, Comma or Percent styles
Currency: £1,565.75   Comma: 1,565.75   Percent: 156575%
Select the cell(s), and click a style tool on the Formatting toolbar.

Chart type

The default chart type is a column chart. You can try out a variety of other chart types using the Chart Type tool on the Standard toolbar.

Basic steps

1 Click the drop-down arrow by the chart types tool to display the types available.

2 Choose one.

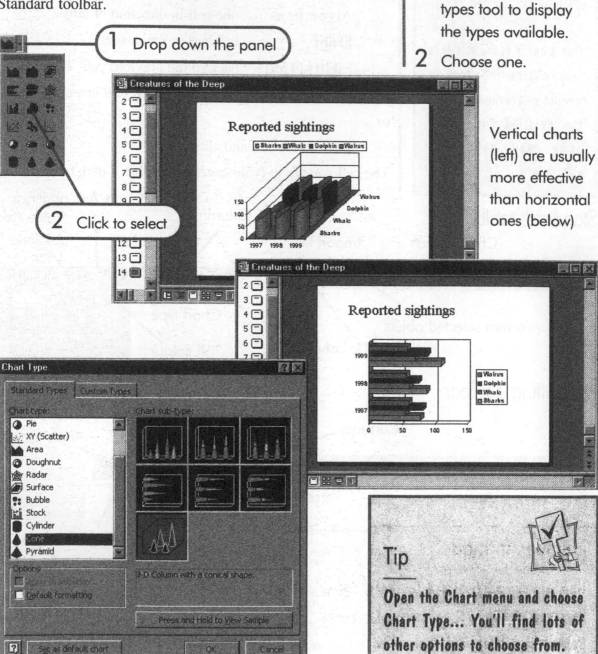

1 Drop down the panel

2 Click to select

Creatures of the Deep

Reported sightings

Vertical charts (left) are usually more effective than horizontal ones (below)

Creatures of the Deep

Reported sightings

Chart Type

Standard Types | Custom Types

Chart type:
- Pie
- XY (Scatter)
- Area
- Doughnut
- Radar
- Surface
- Bubble
- Stock
- Cylinder
- Cone
- Pyramid

Chart sub-type:

3-D Column with a conical shape.

Options
- Apply to selection
- Default formatting

Press and Hold to View Sample

Set as default chart | OK | Cancel

Tip

Open the Chart menu and choose Chart Type... You'll find lots of other options to choose from.

80

Basic steps

1 Display the datasheet if necessary.

2 Double-click on the heading of the column or row you wish to hide.

   The data is dimmed, and is not displayed on your chart.

3 Double-click the heading again to reveal the column or row.

You can customise the basic chart in a number of different ways, to add your own personal touch. Have a look through the menus to see what options are available to you.

Hiding columns

If you don't want all your data to be displayed, you can hide rows or columns as required. This is done on the datasheet.

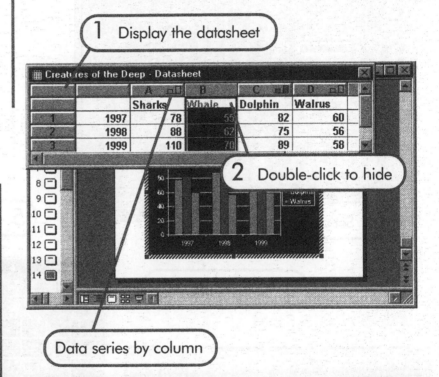

1 Display the datasheet

2 Double-click to hide

Data series by column

Take note

You can easily control which toolbars to display. Right-click on a toolbar that is currently open, and at the list of toolbar names, tick those you wish to display. If you switch all the toolbars off, open the View menu and choose Toolbars to switch them back on again!

Tip

Use the Text Box and Arrow tools on the Drawing toolbar to add emphasis to your charts.

81

Colours and patterns

If you don't like the colour of a data series – the bars representing one set of data on your chart – try experimenting with the options available.

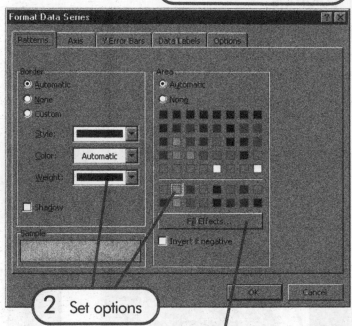

1 Select the data series

2 Set options

3 Click Fill Effects...

1 Double click on a item (e.g. bar or line) in the data series to open the Format Data Series dialog box

2 On the Patterns tab, select the options.

3 If you want a pattern, click Fill Effects...

4 Experiment with the Fill Effects until you find something you like.

5 Click 〖 ok 〗 then 〖 OK 〗 again to exit.

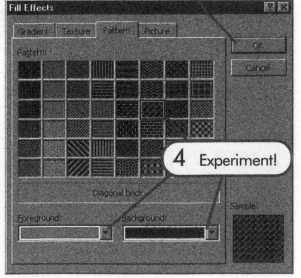

5 Click OK

4 Experiment!

Tip

Select a data series and click the Fill Colour drop-down arrow. Experiment with the colours, or go into the Fill Effects dialog box to get the patterns and textures.

Leaving Graph 2000

When your chart is complete, click anywhere on the slide outside its placeholder to return to your presentation.

When you leave the Graph 2000 environment, the whole chart becomes an object within your presentation, and can be moved, copied, deleted or resized as necessary.

Tip

If you wish to take your chart back into the graphic environment, simply double-click on it.

Name of presentation

Legend

Value axis

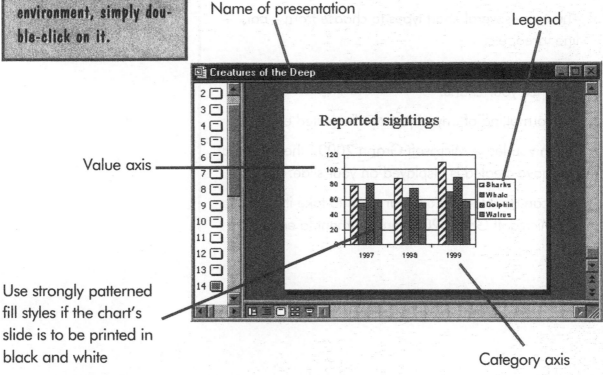

Use strongly patterned fill styles if the chart's slide is to be printed in black and white

Category axis

Tip

Before you leave, look through the menus to see what other options Microsoft Graph 2000 has to offer - there are plenty.

Summary

❑ Charts provide an effective way of displaying data on a slide.

❑ Working in the Microsoft Graph 2000 environment is similar to working and charting in Excel.

❑ The data you wish to chart is entered into a datasheet.

❑ The data series can be in rows or columns.

❑ There are several chart types to choose from – bar, line, area, etc.

❑ Colours, patterns, text and drawing can all be used to enhance your charts.

❑ The formatting of any object can be edited easily.

❑ When you leave Microsoft Graph 2000, the chart that you have created is displayed on your slide.

❑ You can double-click on your chart to take it back into the Microsoft Graph 2000 environment to edit it.

8 More objects...

Organization charts

Organization charts give you another opportunity to make your point using a diagram rather than words.

This section introduces Organization Chart and some of its features. If you use a lot of organization charts, tour through its menus and the on-line Help to appreciate its full potential.

You have a choice on how to get into Organization Chart to set your details up:

● Choose a slide from the New Slide dialog box that has an Organization Chart placeholder on it;

  or

● Choose a slide with an Object placeholder on it.

❑ With an Organization chart placeholder

1 Double-click within the Organization chart placeholder on your slide.

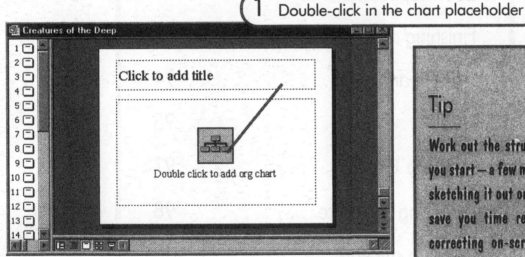

1 Double-click in the chart placeholder

Creatures of the Deep

Click to add title

Double click to add org chart

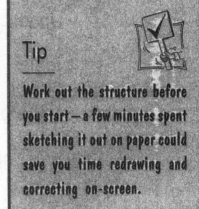

Tip

Work out the structure before you start – a few minutes spent sketching it out on paper could save you time redrawing and correcting on-screen.

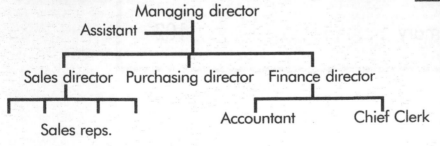

Managing director

Assistant

Sales director Purchasing director Finance director

Sales reps.

Accountant Chief Clerk

The basic structure of the organisation used for the examples in this chapter – see page 94 for the finished chart.

Basic steps

❑ With an object placeholder

1 Double-click within the object placeholder on your slide to open the Insert Object dialog box.

2 Choose MS Organization Chart 2.0.

3 Click [OK].

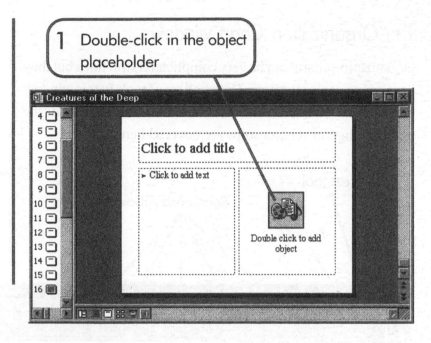

1 Double-click in the object placeholder

Click to add title

Click to add text

Double click to add object

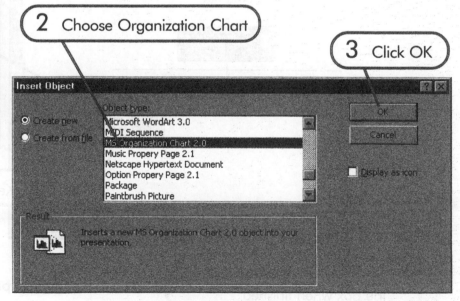

2 Choose Organization Chart

3 Click OK

Insert Object

Object type:
Microsoft WordArt 3.0
MIDI Sequence
MS Organization Chart 2.0
Music Propery Page 2.1
Netscape Hypertext Document
Option Propery Page 2.1
Package
Paintbrush Picture

○ Create new
○ Create from file

OK
Cancel

☐ Display as icon

Result

Inserts a new MS Organization Chart 2.0 object into your presentation.

87

Text and boxes

The Organization Chart window

Organization charts can be very complicated structures but they have only simple elements. The small set of tools in this window are all that you need. Most are for adding boxes, and all the normal range of relationships are covered here.

1 Click in the box you wish to write in.

2 Key in your data and press [Enter] or use the arrow keys to move to the next line in a box.

3 Click on the next box to be completed, or anywhere outside the box, when you are finished.

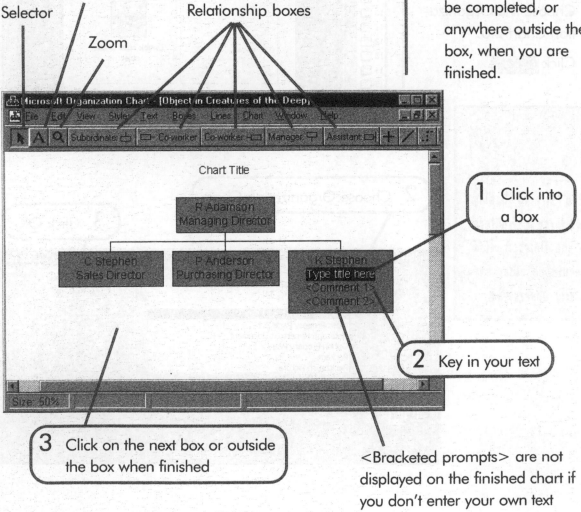

Selector

Text tool

Zoom

Relationship boxes

1 Click into a box

2 Key in your text

3 Click on the next box or outside the box when finished

<Bracketed prompts> are not displayed on the finished chart if you don't enter your own text

88

Adding and deleting boxes

You can easily build your chart up by adding boxes where needed. Deleting boxes is even easier.

● You can add several boxes simultaneously – see the Tip below.

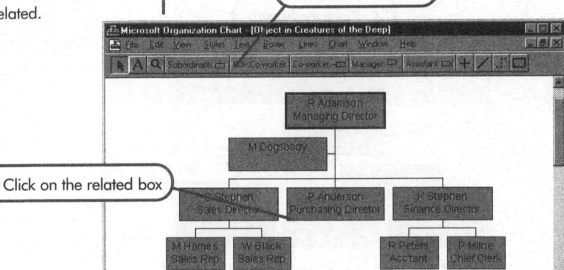

1 Select a box type

2 Click on the related box

Microsoft Organization Chart - [Object in Creatures of the Deep]

File Edit View Styles Text Boxes Lines Chart Window Help

Subordinate Co-worker Co-worker Manager Assistant

R Adamson
Managing Director

M Dogsbody

S Stephen
Sales Director

P Anderson
Purchasing Director

K Stephen
Finance Director

M Hames
Sales Rep

W Black
Sales Rep

R Peters
Acc'tant

P Milne
Chief Clerk

Size 50%

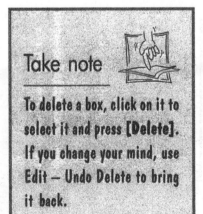

Take note

To delete a box, click on it to select it and press [Delete]. If you change your mind, use Edit – Undo Delete to bring it back.

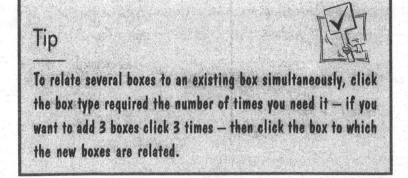

Tip

To relate several boxes to an existing box simultaneously, click the box type required the number of times you need it – if you want to add 3 boxes click 3 times – then click the box to which the new boxes are related.

Text and drawing tools

The text and drawing tools can be used to add the finishing touches to your organization chart. If you need text outside the boxes on your chart, use the Text tool.

❏ Text

1 Click the Text tool A.

2 Click to position the insertion point.

3 Key in the text.

4 Click anywhere outside the text area to deselect the text.

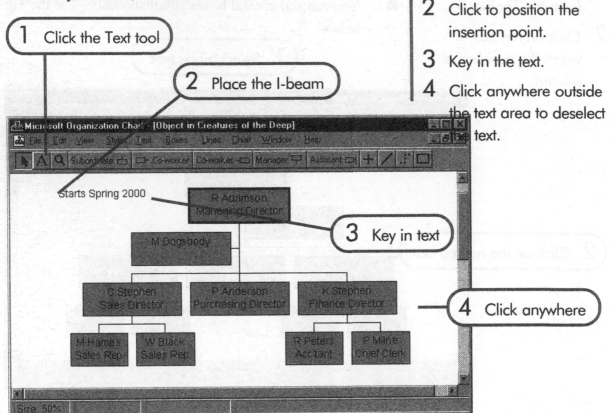

1 Click the Text tool

2 Place the I-beam

3 Key in text

4 Click anywhere

The Drawing tools

There are four drawing tools – three types of line and a box. These are all you need to build an organization chart.

❏ Drawing

5 Select a tool.

6 Click and drag to draw a line or box.

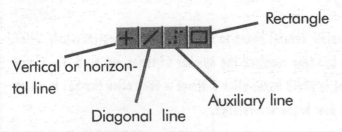

Rectangle

Vertical or horizontal line

Diagonal line

Auxiliary line

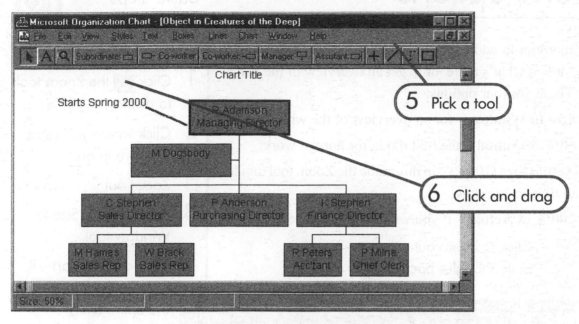

□ Chart title

7 Select the Chart Title prompt.

8 Key in the title.

or

Press [Delete] to remove the prompt.

Chart title

You can give your chart a title here or in the Slide Title area, back in your presentation. If you opt to key in the title in the presentation, delete the Chart Title prompt.

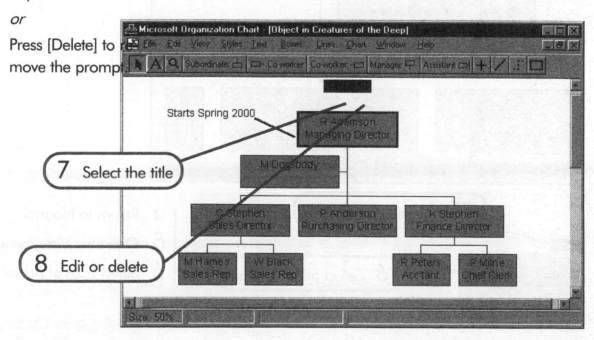

Zoom options

You can zoom in and out on your organization chart to get a closer look at what's there, or to get an overview of the whole thing. There are four options:

- **Size to Window** – for an overview of the whole chart;

- **50% of Actual** – the best mode for normal work;

- **Actual Size** (100%) – in this mode the Zoom tool toggles to Size to Window;

- **200% of Actual** – if you want to get really close.

Click to Zoom out – the button toggles back to 🔍

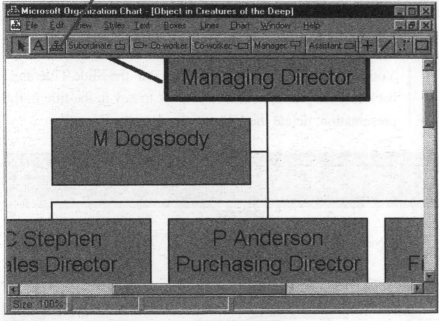

5 Open the View menu

6 Select 50% of Actual

Basic steps

❑ Zoom to Actual size

1 Click 🔍 the Zoom tool to display at 100%

2 Click where you want to zoom in on.

❑ Zoom out

3 Select 🔳 the Size to Window tool.

4 Click on the chart – it reduces so you can see the entire chart.

❑ Return to Normal

5 Open the View menu.

6 Select 50% of Actual.

92

Basic steps

❑ To restyle a box

1 Select the box(es).

2 Open the Boxes menu and choose Border, Shadow or Color.

3 Select an option.

❑ To edit lines

4 Select the line(s).

5 From the Lines menu choose Thickness, Style or Color.

6 Select an option.

Using the Boxes, Lines and Text menus, you can add the finishing touches to your organisation chart – edit the line styles, add shadows to the boxes, change the colour, size and font of text, etc.

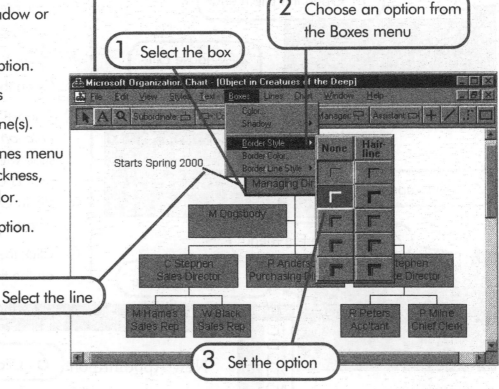

2 Choose an option from the Boxes menu

1 Select the box

4 Select the line

3 Set the option

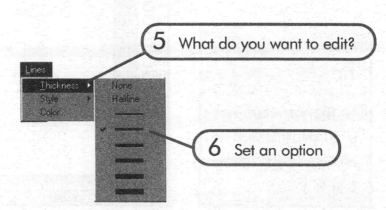

5 What do you want to edit?

6 Set an option

Tip

To select several boxes or lines at once, select one then hold [Shift], and click on the others.

Update and exit

Once you've completed your organisation chart, you will need to update the slide in your presentation and return to the presentation proper to continue working on it. Exit Organization Chart as you do any Windows application.

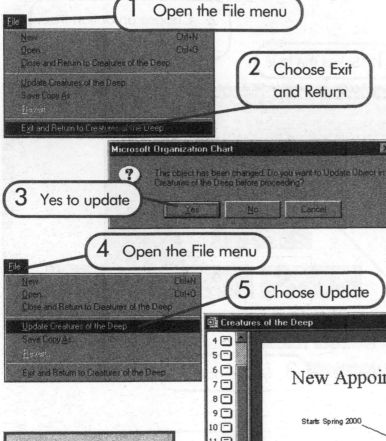

1 Open the File menu

2 Choose Exit and Return

3 Yes to update

4 Open the File menu

5 Choose Update

Basic steps

1 Open the File menu.

2 Choose Exit and Return to *presentation name.*

3 Click Yes to update your presentation, before exiting.

or

4 Open the File menu.

5 Choose Update *presentation name.* Your slide will now display your chart, but you are still in Organization Chart.

6 Click the Close button on the title bar.

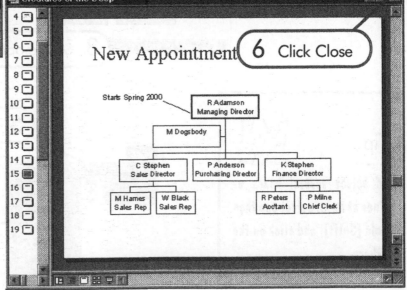

6 Click Close

Tip

To take your chart back into Organization Chart for editing, simply double-click on it.

Basic steps

- ❑ Slide with placeholder
- 1 Double click on the table placeholder on your slide.
- 2 Specify the number of rows and columns.
- 3 Click ▭ OK ▭.
- 4 Complete the table as shown on the next page.

Take note

When working on a table, you will notice a Table menu appear on your menu bar.

Take note

[Tab]	move to the next cell
[Shift]-[Tab]	move to the previous cell
[Arrow keys]	move up, down, right and left

Click in the cell you wish to work on.

If you are accustomed to creating tables using Word, you'll find it very easy to create tables on your slides. A table is inserted as an object.

There are several ways to get started. You could:

- ● Create a new slide with a table placeholder set up;
- ● Draw your table onto the slide;
- ● Use the Insert Word Table tool on the standard toolbar.

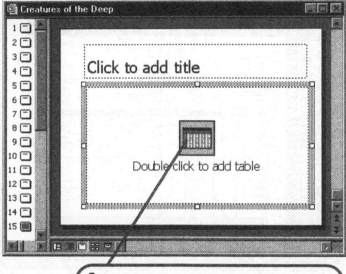

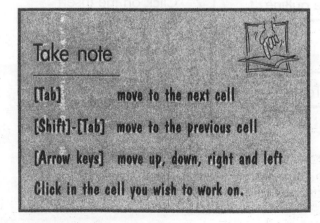

1 Double-click in the placeholder

2 Set the table size

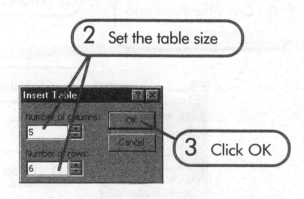

3 Click OK

Tables and borders toolbar

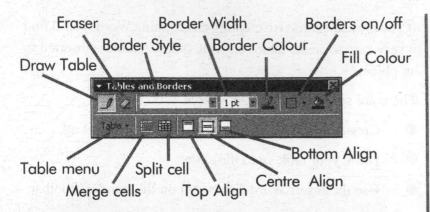

Eraser — Border Width — Borders on/off

Border Style — Border Colour

Draw Table — Fill Colour

Table menu — Split cell — Bottom Align

Merge cells — Top Align — Centre Align

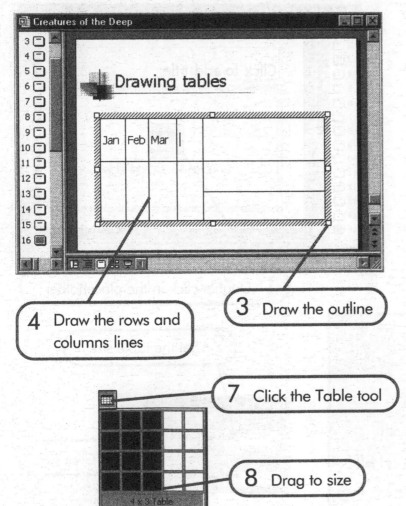

4 Draw the rows and columns lines

3 Draw the outline

7 Click the Table tool

8 Drag to size

Basic steps

❏ To draw your table

1 Click the Tables and Borders tool 🔲 to display the Tables and Borders toolbar.

2 Select the Draw Table tool 📝.

3 Click and drag to draw the table outline.

4 Draw lines to create the rows and columns.

❏ To remove a line:

5 Select the Eraser 🔲 and click on the line.

6 Switch the Draw Table tool off – click 📝 or press [Esc].

❏ From a slide with no Table placeholder

7 Click on the Insert Table tool on the Standard toolbar.

8 Click and drag over the grid to specify the table size required.

9 Complete your table.

Basic steps

❑ From a slide with Clip Art placeholder

1 Double-click within the Clip art placeholder.

❑ From a slide with an Object placeholder

2 Double-click within the object placeholder to open the Insert Object dialog box.

3 Choose Microsoft Clip Gallery.

4 Click OK.

❑ From a slide with no placeholder set

5 Click the Insert Clip Art tool on the Standard toolbar.

PowerPoint comes with hundreds of Clip art pictures that can be added to your slides. In addition to the clips that come with PowerPoint 2000, you'll find that you can access many more on the Internet.

There are three main ways of adding Clip Art – all take you to the Clip Gallery.

● Set up a New Slide with a Clip Art placeholder on it;

● Choose a slide with an Object placeholder already on it;

● Click the Insert Clip Art tool.

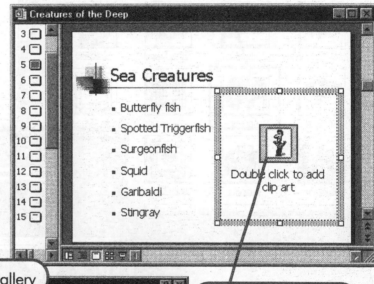

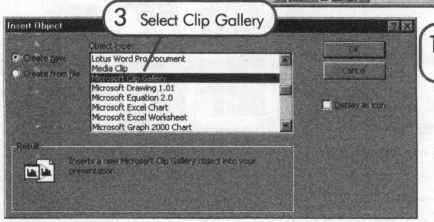

Choosing a picture

The Clip Art is organised into several categories to make it easier for you to locate pictures. Browse through them to see what is available. Once you have selected the category, thumbnail images are displayed in the preview window. Simply choose the one that best suits your purposes.

Basic steps

1 Click on a Category.

2 Scroll through the Pictures until you see the one you want.

3 Click on a picture to select it.

4 Preview the picture if you want a closer look.

5 Click Insert clip or ▭ OK or double-click on a picture to place it on your slide.

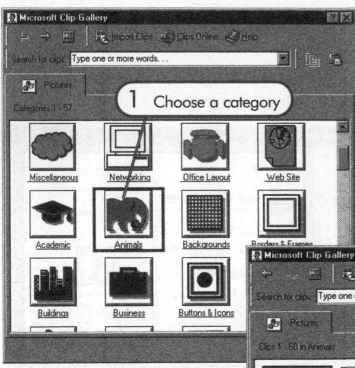

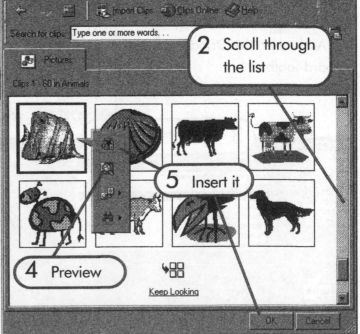

Tip

If you have Internet Access, you can download pictures, sound and movie clips from the Clip Gallery Web site — click Clips Online to go to it.

Basic steps

1 Enter a keyword in the Search for clips field and press [Enter].

2 Refine your search if necessary.

3 If you locate a clip you will use again, add it to the Favorites category.

Searching for pictures

Rather than scroll through the lists of pictures, you may find it quicker to search for the type of picture you are looking for.

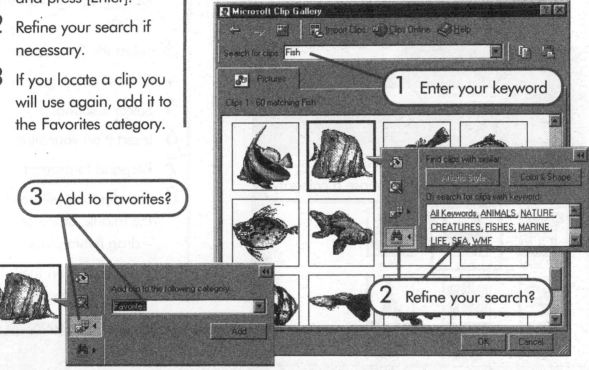

1 Enter your keyword

3 Add to Favorites?

2 Refine your search?

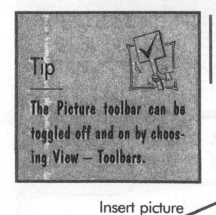
Fine tuning the picture

Pictures can be edited in the same way as other objects. You can also use the tools on the Picture toolbar to create special effects.

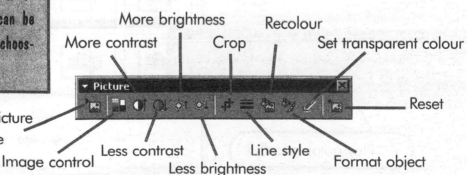

More brightness

More contrast

Crop

Recolour

Set transparent colour

Reset

Insert picture from file

Image control

Less contrast

Less brightness

Line style

Format object

Music to my ears

There are several short pieces of music supplied with Office that you may find useful in a presentation (usually at the beginning or the end) or you could include something from your own CDs.

Basic steps

1 Go to the desired slide.

2 Click the Insert Clip Art tool on the Drawing toolbar.

3 Select the Sounds tab.

4 Choose a category.

5 Select a sound.

6 Insert it on your slide.

7 Respond to prompt.

8 The clip icon will be in the middle of the slide – drag it into place.

❑ Double-click on the icon to play the sound.

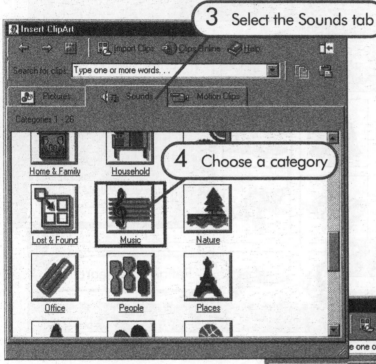

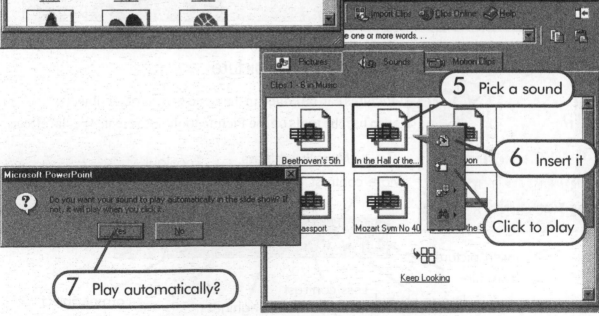

100

Basic steps

1 Insert your CD into the CD drive. If it starts to play, stop it and close the CD dialog box.

2 From the Insert menu choose Movies and Sounds, then Play CD Audio Track.

3 Set the Start and End track.

4 Click [OK].

5 Respond to the play sound prompt.

❑ In your presentation:

To play the track(s), click on the icon.

To stop playing, press [Esc].

To edit the settings for an audio or video object, right click on it and choose Edit Sound (or Movie) Object from the shortcut menu. Complete the dialog box as required.

Music from a CD

You can also select a clip from one of your own CDs.

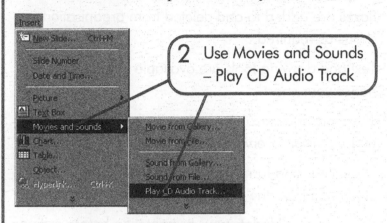

2 Use Movies and Sounds – Play CD Audio Track

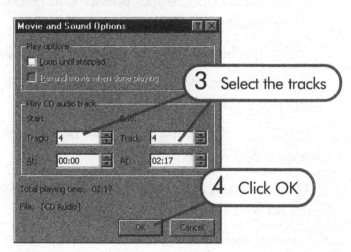

3 Select the tracks

4 Click OK

Video clips

You can add video clips to your presentation in the same way – choose **Movie from Gallery** from the **Movies and Sounds** submenu, or select the **Motion Clips** tab in the **Insert Clip Art** dialog box.

Summary

❑ Organization Charts can easily be added to slides.

❑ Boxes are added to and deleted from organisation charts as required.

❑ Text and drawing tools are available to further enhance your chart.

❑ There are several Zoom options so you can get a close up look or an overview of your chart.

❑ The colour and format of items on your chart can be controlled from the Boxes and Text menus.

❑ Remember to Update your presentation before exiting Organization Chart.

❑ Tables can be created on your slides very easily.

❑ The simplest way to add Clip Art is to start with a slide that has a Clip Art placeholder.

❑ The Clip Gallery contains pictures, photographs, sounds and movies.

❑ You can move, resize or delete the Clip Art object once it is on your slide.

❑ You can easily add CD or other sound clips, or video clips into your presentation.

9 Masters

Slide Master

The Slide Master holds the formatted placeholders for the slide title and text. Changes to the Slide Master will be reflected in every slide in your presentation (except the Title Slide). Any slides where you have made changes to the text formatting at slide level will be treated as exceptions and will retain the custom formatting you applied to them.

Any background objects you want to appear on every slide (like your company name or logo) should be added to the Slide Master.

1 Choose Master from the View menu.

2 Select Slide Master.

3 Amend the Slide Master as required (using the same techniques you use on a slide in your presentation).

4 Choose an alternative view to leave your Slide Master.

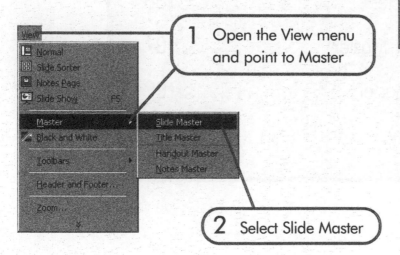

1 Open the View menu and point to Master

2 Select Slide Master

Tip

If you hold down [Shift] and click ▣ the Slide View icon, this takes you to the Slide Master, or to the Title Master (page 106) if you are on the title slide at the time.

Take note

The title slide has its own master. Changes made to the Slide Master will not be reflected on your title slide.

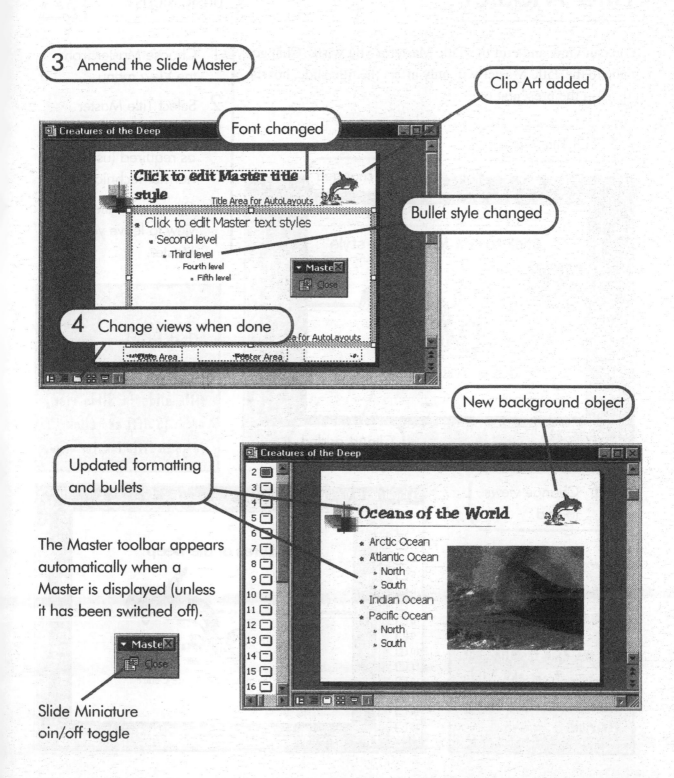

3 Amend the Slide Master

Clip Art added

Font changed

Creatures of the Deep

Click to edit Master title style
Title Area for AutoLayouts

Bullet style changed

* Click to edit Master text styles
  * Second level
    * Third level
      Fourth level
      * Fifth level

▼ Master ✕
📇 Close

4 Change views when done

a for AutoLayouts

Date Area   Footer Area   -#-

New background object

Updated formatting and bullets

Creatures of the Deep

Oceans of the World

* Arctic Ocean
* Atlantic Ocean
  * North
  * South
* Indian Ocean
* Pacific Ocean
  * North
  * South

The Master toolbar appears automatically when a Master is displayed (unless it has been switched off).

▼ Master ✕
📇 Close

Slide Miniature oin/off toggle

105

Title Master

You can view and edit the Title Master if you wish. Changes made to the Title Master will only affect the title slide, not the others in the presentation.

Basic steps

1 Choose Master from the View menu.

2 Select Title Master.

3 Amend the Title Master as required (using the normal techniques).

4 Choose an alternative view to leave your Title Master.

3 Edit Title Master

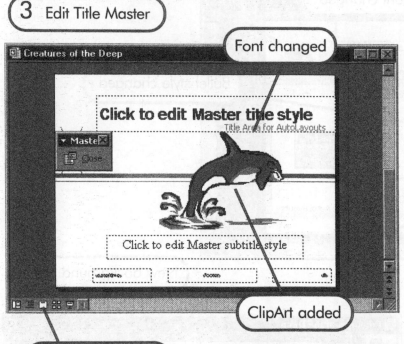

Font changed

Click to edit Master title style

Title Area for AutoLayouts

Click to edit Master subtitle style

ClipArt added

4 Change views to end

Take note

If you are looking at the title slide in Slide view, press [Shift] and click ⬜ to go to Title Master view.

Tip

You can drag the slide bar to move from the Slide Master to the Title Master view.

Creatures of the Deep

Creatures of the Deep

Edinburgh Sea Life Centre

Basic steps

1 Choose Master from the View menu.

2 Select Handout Master.

3 Select 2, 3, 4, 6 or 9 slides to the page.

4 Add Clip Art if wanted.

5 Choose Header and Footer from the View menu.

6 Edit the Header and/or Footer text if necessary and click [Apply to All].

7 Choose an alternative view to leave your Handout Master.

You can support your presentation with audience handouts if you wish. Handouts consist of smaller, printed versions of your slides, either 2, 3, 4, 6 or 9 pages (see Chapter 11 for details on printing).

If you want additional information on the handout pages – your company name or logo, the presentation title, page numbers, date, or lines for your audience to write on – add the detail to the Handout Master.

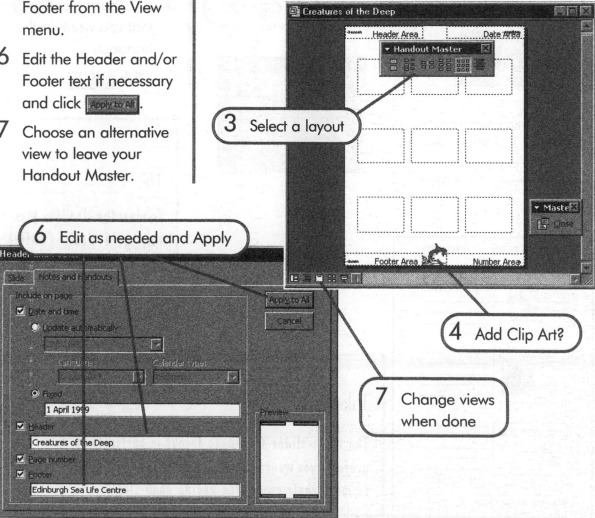

3 Select a layout

6 Edit as needed and Apply

4 Add Clip Art?

7 Change views when done

The placeholders

The Date, Page Number, Header or Footer placeholders are all optional. They can easily be deleted – or put back again if you decide you want them after all. Print a copy of your handouts and see how they look on paper before making a final decision.

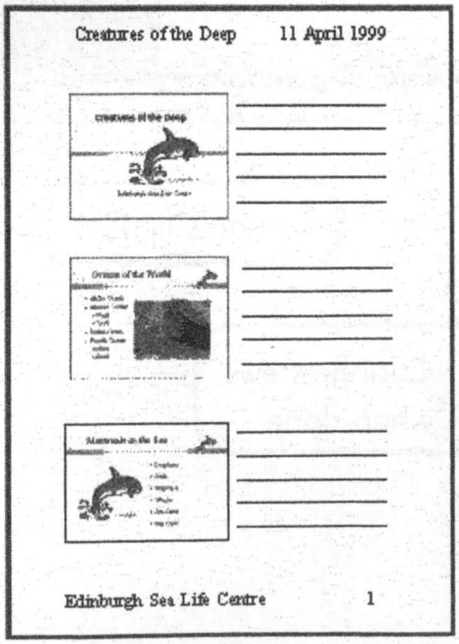

Basic steps

- ❏ Deleting placeholders
1 Select the placeholder and press [Delete].
- ❏ Restoring placeholders
2 Select Handout Master Layout from the Common Tasks list.
3 Tick those placeholders that you want on the handouts.
4 Click OK .

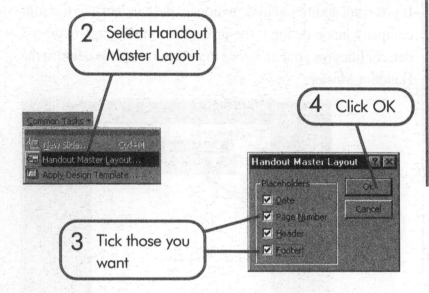

2 Select Handout Master Layout

4 Click OK

3 Tick those you want

Tip

To view the Handout Master, hold down [Shift] and click either the Outline view or the Slide Sorter view icon.

Take note

The three-slides-to-a-page layout is particularly useful if you want to leave space for your audience to make their own notes beside each slide.

1 Choose Master from the View menu.

2 Select Notes Master.

3 Amend the Notes Master as required.

4 Choose an alternative view to leave your Notes Master.

Each slide in your presentation has an accompanying notes page which consists of a smaller version of the slide along with room for any notes you want to make.

If you want to add information to your notes pages (company name or page number perhaps), or change the size of the placeholders (to allow more space for notes and less for the slide image) do so on the Notes Master.

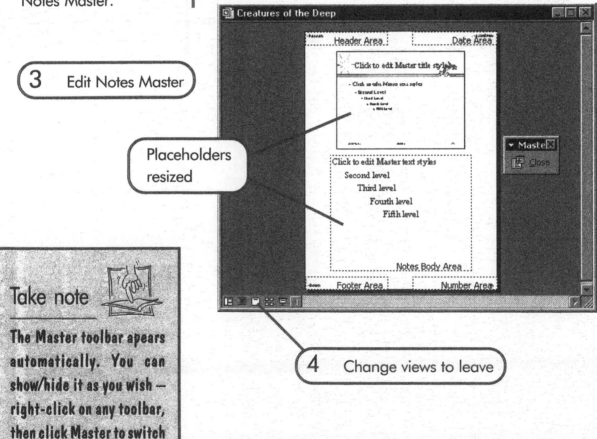

3 Edit Notes Master

Placeholders resized

4 Change views to leave

Take note

The Master toolbar apears automatically. You can show/hide it as you wish — right-click on any toolbar, then click Master to switch it on or off.

Summary

❑ If you want to add or amend an element to every slide (except the title slide) in your presentation, change the Slide Master, not the individual slides.

❑ If you want to add or amend an element to the Title slide, change the Title Master, not the individual slide.

❑ Text, graphics, page numbers, time and date fields added to the Slide, Handout and Notes Masters appear on every slide or page.

❑ Hold the [Shift] key down when you click the View icons to get the Masters.

10 Slide shows

Slide Sorter view

There are several useful features worth exploring in Slide Sorter view, including:

- Hiding slides;
- Setting up transitions;
- Animating text on slides;
- Rehearsing timings;

We'll look at these features in this section, and see how they can help enhance your presentations.

You should be in Slide Sorter view for this section.

> **Take note**
>
> The topics introduced in this chapter are only useful if you will be giving on-screen presentations (slide shows). They do not apply to overheads and 35mm slides.

Slide Sorter toolbar

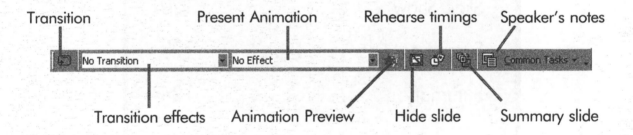

Transition — Present Animation — Rehearse timings — Speaker's notes

Transition effects — Animation Preview — Hide slide — Summary slide

> **Take note**
>
> Transitions, Text Animation and Hiding Slides can be specified in any view using the Slide Show menu, but I find it easiest to do them from Slide Sorter view using the Slide Sorter toolbar.

Basic steps

1 Select the slide you want to hide.

2 Click the Hide Slide tool.

❑ The number is crossed out under the slide.

This option can prove useful if you're not sure whether or not you will really need a particular slide for your presentation. You can include the slide in your presentation (in case it's needed), but hide it. The hidden slide will be bypassed during your slide show, unless you decide you need to use it.

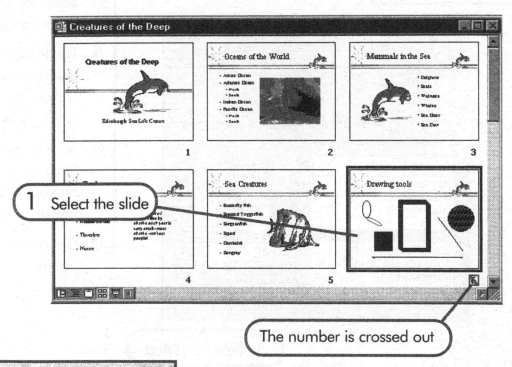

1 Select the slide

The number is crossed out

Tip

If you want to show the hidden slide during a presentation, use the Go To command, or press [H] at the slide preceding the hidden one.

Take note

To remove the hidden status from a slide, select it and click the Hide Slide tool again.

Transitions

A transition is an effect used between slides in a show. The default option is that No Transition is set, but there are some interesting alternatives you might find effective for your presentation. Experiment with the Transition options to find those best suited to your presentation.

Basic steps

1 Select the slide to which you want to specify a transition.

2 Click the Slide Transition tool on the Slide Sorter toolbar

3 Select the Effect from the drop down list.

4 The Preview window demonstrates the effect – click on it to see the effect again.

5 Set the Speed to Fast. Focus your audiences on your slides, not the transition method!

6 Choose an Advance option.

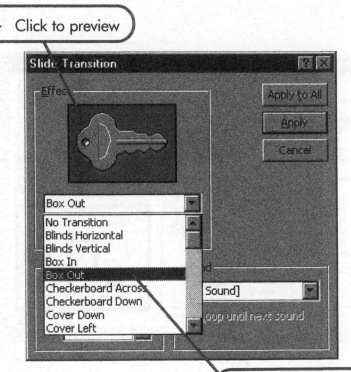

4 Click to preview

3 Select an Effect

Take note

If you wish, you can use the Advance option in the Transition dialog box to set slide timings manually (rather than through Rehearse Timings, see page 118).

7 Add a Sound if wanted.

8 Click Apply or Apply to All if you want the effect added to all your slides.

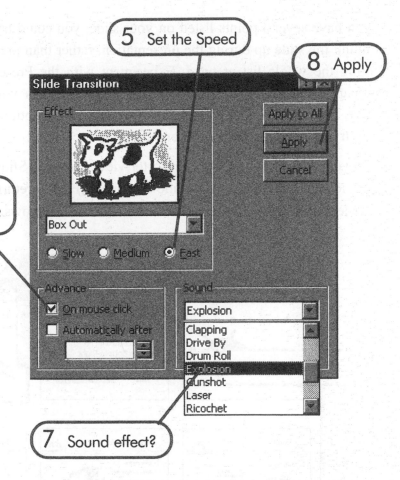

5 Set the Speed

8 Apply

6 Automatic or mouse Advance?

7 Sound effect?

Take note

If a transition is set, a transition icon appears below the slide in Slide Sorter view. Click on it to see the transition effect. You can also preview a transition by selecting the slide, then clicking the Animation Preview tool on the Slide Sorter toolbar.

Tip

Use the Slide Show together with Slide Sorter view when experimenting with animation effects. Then you can check that the options you choose are having the desired effect. See page 120 for more on Slide Shows.

Preset animations

If you have several points listed on your slide, you could try building the slide up during the presentation, rather than presenting the whole list at once. Experiment with the Preset Animation options and effects until you find the ones you prefer. You can have a lot of fun messing about with the options – but try to avoid having a different effect on each slide!

With your slide selected in Slide Sorter view, click the Slide Show icon, work through your slide then press [Esc] to return to Slide Sorter view. See page 120 for more on slide shows.

Basic steps

1 Select the slide.

2 Drop down the Preset Animation list on the Slide Sorter toolbar.

3 Choose an effect.

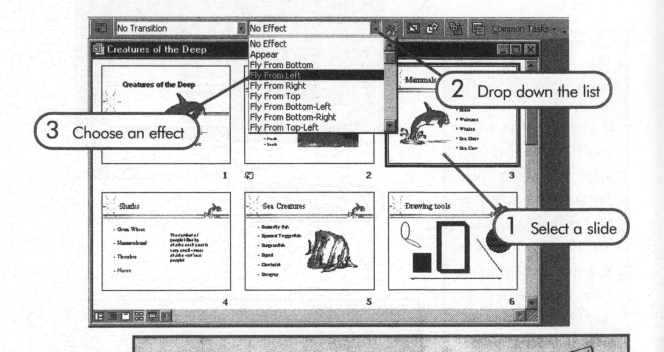

Tip

You can preview your animation effects in Normal, Slide or Outline view. Display the slide with animations, then choose Animation Preview from the Slide Show menu. The animation effects will be displayed in a slide miniature.

Basic steps

1 Select the slide (or slides) you wish to animate.

2 Choose Preset Animation from the Slide Show menu.

3 Select the option required.

Animation from the Slide Show menu

You can also set up your animation options through the Slide Show menu – you may find it simpler to work through these more organised menus.

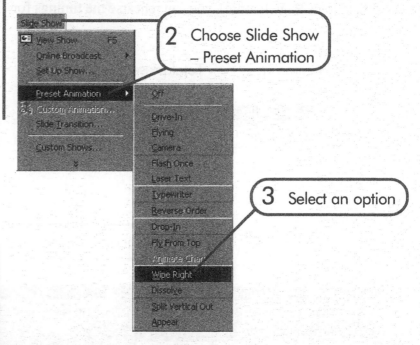

Take note

You can set up your own animations (rather than use the preset ones) if you wish. In Normal, Slide or Outline view, open the Slide Show menu and choose Custom Animation. Experiment with the options to see what effects you can create.

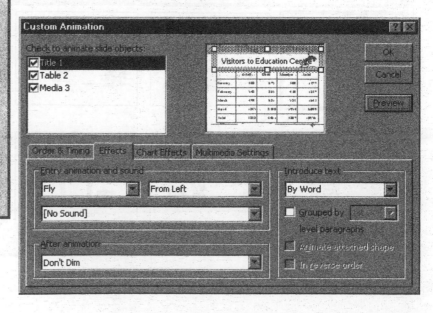

Rehearse Timings

It is a very good idea to practise your presentation before you end up in front of your audience. As well as practising what you intend to say (probably with the aid of notes you have made using the Notes Page feature), you can rehearse the timings for each slide.

Slide time   Total presentation time

Next —

Pause   Repeat

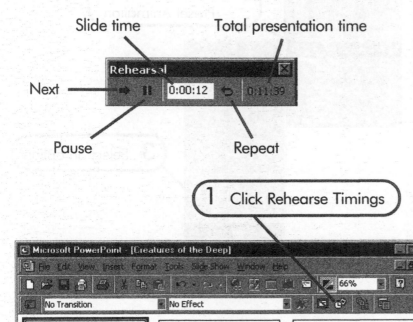

1   Click Rehearse Timings

Basic steps

1 Click the Rehearse Timings tool to go into your slide show for a practice run!

2 Go over what you intend to say while the slide is displayed.

3 Click the left mouse button to move to the next slide when ready.

4 Repeat steps 2 and 3 until you reach the end of your presentation.

Tip

You can set your timings manually in the Slide Transition dialog box. See page 115.

118

Displaying timings

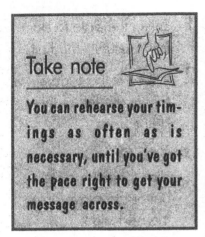

Take note

You can rehearse your timings as often as is necessary, until you've got the pace right to get your message across.

A dialog box displays the total length of time your presentation took and asks if you want to record and use the new slide timings in a slide show. Choose 'Yes', if you want each slide to advance after the allocated time (useful if you want to leave the presentation running in youre absence) or 'No' if someone is going to front it in person.

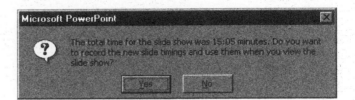

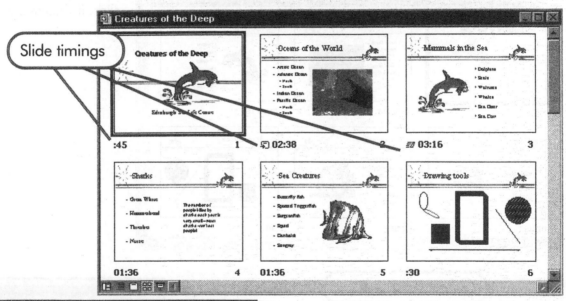

Slide timings

Tip

Click the [icon] Speaker's Notes tool to view/edit the notes for the selected slide.

Slide Show

You can run your slide show at any time to check how your presentation is progressing. Each slide fills the whole of your computer screen.

After the last, you are returned to the view you were in when you clicked the Slide Show tool.

Basic steps

1 Select the slide to start from, usually the first.

2 Click the Slide Show tool to the left of the status bar.

3 Press [PageDown] (or click the left mouse button) to move onto the next slide.

Press [PageUp] to move back to the previous slide if necessary.

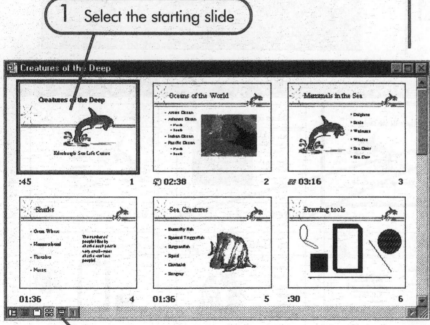

1 Select the starting slide

2 Click Slide Show

Take note

You can exit your slide show at any time by pressing the [Esc] key on your keyboard.

Basic steps

1 Click the right mouse button or the pop-up menu icon at the bottom left corner of the screen.

❑ To go directly to a slide

2 Select Go, then By Title.

3 Choose the slide you want to go to.

Working within your slide show

When presenting your slide show, you might want to leave the normal sequence, go directly to a slide, or draw on the slide to focus attention. These, and other features can be accessed using the pop-up menu or the keyboard.

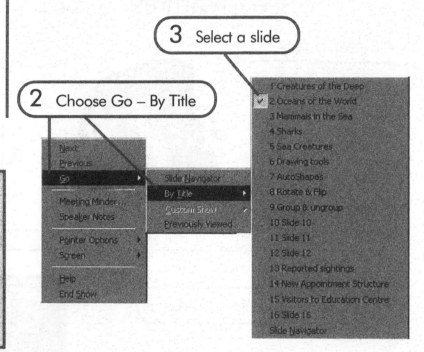

3 Select a slide

2 Choose Go – By Title

Next	
Previous	
Go ▶	Slide Navigator
	By Title ▶
Meeting Minder...	Custom Show
Speaker Notes	Previously Viewed
Pointer Options ▶	
Screen ▶	
Help	
End Show	

1 Creatures of the Deep
2 Oceans of the World ✓
3 Mammals in the Sea
4 Sharks
5 Sea Creatures
6 Drawing tools
7 AutoShapes
8 Rotate & Flip
9 Group & ungroup
10 Slide 10
11 Slide 11
12 Slide 12
13 Reported sightings
14 New Appointment Structure
15 Visitors to Education Centre
16 Slide 16
Slide Navigator

Tip

Experiment with the pop-up menu to see what options are available.

Take note

You can Blackout your screen by pressing [B] or Whiteout your screen by pressing [W]. This could prove useful while you explain something, or show your audience something. Simply press [B] or [W] again to restore the Slide view.

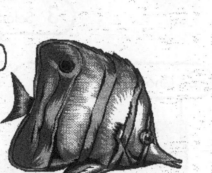

2   Drag the pointer to draw

Sea Creatures

- Butterfly fish
- Spotted Triggerfish
- Surgeonfish
- Squid
- Garibaldi
- Stingray

Click to open the control panel

❑ To 'draw' on the slides

1   Press [Ctrl]-[P] to change the mouse pointer to a pen.

2   Click and drag to draw.

3   Press [Ctrl]-[A] to change the mouse pointer back to an arrow shape when you've finished.

❑ To erase your drawing

4   Press [E] on your keyboard.

Take note

To get more help on the options available while running a slide show, press [F1]. The Slide Show Help dialog box lists other options you might want to experiment with.

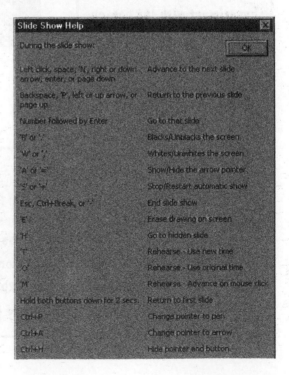

Slide Show Help	OK
During the slide show:	
Left click, space, 'N', right or down arrow, enter, or page down	Advance to the next slide
Backspace, 'P', left or up arrow, or page up	Return to the previous slide
Number followed by Enter	Go to that slide
'B' or '.'	Blacks/Unblacks the screen
'W' or ','	Whites/Unwhites the screen
'A' or '='	Show/Hide the arrow pointer
'S' or '+'	Stop/Restart automatic show
Esc, Ctrl+Break, or '-'	End slide show
'E'	Erase drawing on screen
'H'	Go to hidden slide
'T'	Rehearse - Use new time
'O'	Rehearse - Use original time
'M'	Rehearse - Advance on mouse click
Hold both buttons down for 2 secs.	Return to first slide
Ctrl+P	Change pointer to pen
Ctrl+A	Change pointer to arrow
Ctrl+H	Hide pointer and button

Basic steps

1 Hold [Shift] and click to select the slides you wish to produce a Summary Slide from.

2 Click ⊞ the Summary Slide tool on the Slide Sorter toolbar.

You can get PowerPoint to automatically produce a Summary Slide for your presentation. The Summary Slide is placed in front of the other slides in your presentation. PowerPoint takes the title of each slide you select and lists it on the Summary Slide.

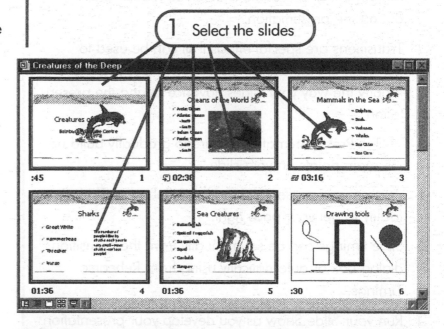

1 Select the slides

Tip

To select multiple slides, hold [Shift] down and click on each in turn.

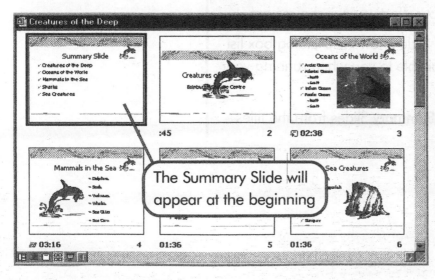

The Summary Slide will appear at the beginning

Take note

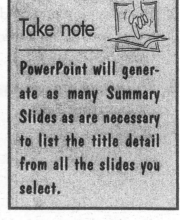

PowerPoint will generate as many Summary Slides as are necessary to list the title detail from all the slides you select.

Summary

❑ Slide Sorter view can be useful when preparing a slide show for presentation on your computer, as well as for moving your slides around.

❑ Slides that you may not need can be Hidden, but remain easily accessible should you require them during the presentation.

❑ Transitions are special effects that can be used to introduce a slide during a slide show. Use them to modify the way your slides advance during the presentation.

❑ Try the Preset Animation feature to gradually build up the main points on your slide.

❑ Practise your presentation with the Rehearse Timings facility to get your pace right.

❑ Slide timings can be set manually from the Transition dialog box or automatically using from Rehearse Timings.

❑ Run your Slide Show as you develop your presentation – it'll help you check how effective your choices are.

❑ The pop-up menu and Slide Show Help dialog box list the various options available to you when running your slide show.

❑ PowerPoint can create Summary Slides from the titles of your other slides.

11 Printing presentations

Slide format

You can print your whole presentation in PowerPoint - the slides, speaker's notes pages, audience handouts and the presentation outline.

You can print copies of your slides onto paper or onto overhead transparencies, or you can create slides using a desktop film recorder, or get a bureau to create the slides for you.

The first stage to printing your presentation is to set up the slide format.

Basic steps

1 Choose Page Setup from the File menu.

2 Select the size from the Slides sized for field.

3 Specify the orientation required for the Slides.

4 Specify the orientation required for the Notes, handouts & outline.

5 Click OK.

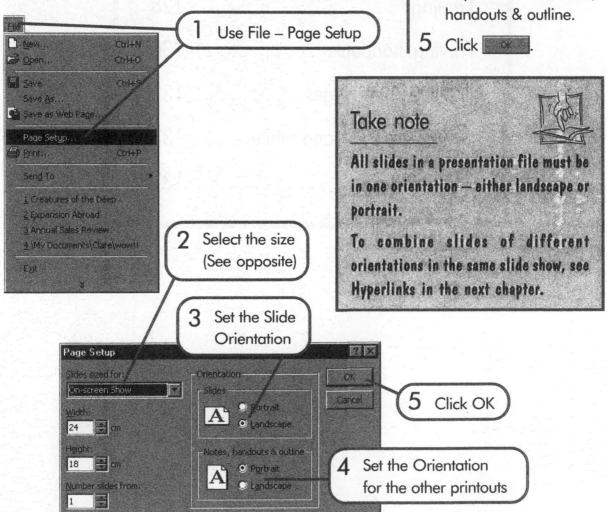

1 Use File – Page Setup

2 Select the size (See opposite)

3 Set the Slide Orientation

4 Set the Orientation for the other printouts

5 Click OK

Take note

All slides in a presentation file must be in one orientation — either landscape or portrait.

To combine slides of different orientations in the same slide show, see Hyperlinks in the next chapter.

Options in the Slide sized for list:

Type	Width	Height
On-screen show	24 cm	18 cm
Letter Paper	24 cm	18 cm
A4 Paper	26 cm	18 cm
35mm Slides	27 cm	18 cm
Overhead	24 cm	18 cm
Banner	19.2 cm	2.4 cm
Custom	set own measurements	

Example of Letter Paper size, portrait orientation

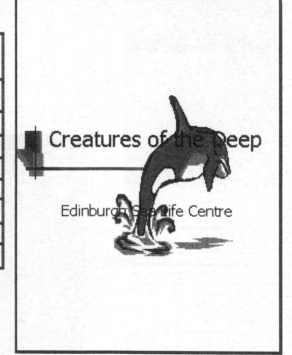

Example of Banner, landscape orientation

Printing

With the Slide Setup details specified to give the output required, you can go ahead and print your slides, handouts, notes pages or the outline.

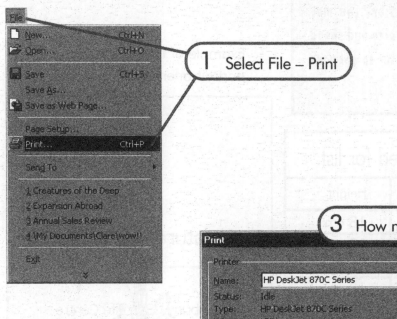

1 Select File – Print

1 Open the File menu and choose Print.

2 Specify the Print range to print.

3 Set the Number of copies, if required.

4 Select one of the Slide options from the Print What: list.

5 Click [OK].

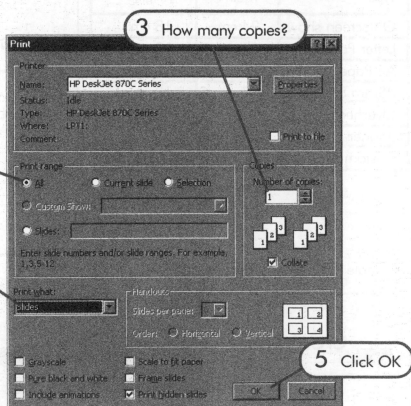

3 How many copies?

2 Set the range

4 Set the option

5 Click OK

Print what: options

Slides

Prints your slides on paper or overhead transparencies, one slide per page.

Handouts

Prints miniatures of the slides 2, 3, 4, 6, or 9 to the page. Printing your handouts with 3 slides to the page is particularly useful as there is room for your audience to make their own notes, see page 131.

Notes Page

A slide miniature is printed, together with any notes that you have made to prompt you during your presentation. See page 132.

Outline View

The text of each slide is printed out, showing the structure of the presentation.

Tip

You can specify your print range in Slide Sorter view. Select the slides you wish to print from Slide Sorter view (click on the first one, then [Shift]-click on each additional slide), then in the print range options of the Print dialog box, choose Selection.

Take note

If you are going to send your slides to a service bureau to be turned into 35 mm slides or other materials, contact the bureau first for any specific requirements on the file formats.

Printing handouts

You can print copies of your slides out to issue as audience handouts. The format of the handout can be set up to include 2, 3, 4, 6 or 9 slides to the page.

If you want to add text, Clip Art, etc. to your handouts, you must edit the Handouts Master page.

Handouts and Notes Pages are usually printed in grayscale or black and white (see page 133)

(see page 133)

1 Choose Print from the File menu.

2 Select Handouts (2 , 3, 4, 6 or 9 slides per page as required).

3 Set the Print range.

4 Click OK.

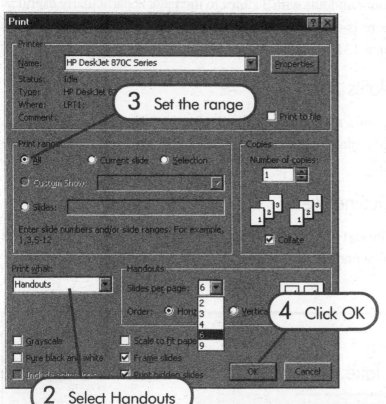

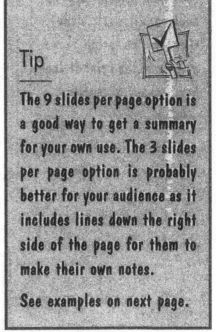

Tip

The 9 slides per page option is a good way to get a summary for your own use. The 3 slides per page option is probably better for your audience as it includes lines down the right side of the page for them to make their own notes.

See examples on next page.

See examples on next page.

Take note

You can print Hidden slides on your handouts, even if you skip them during the presentation.

Handout printed 6 slides to a page

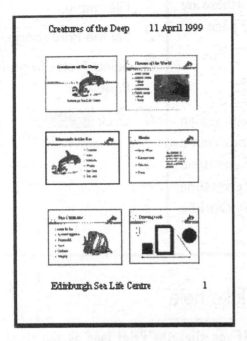

Handout printed 2 slides to a page

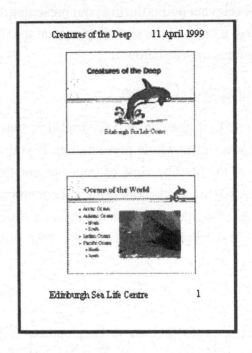

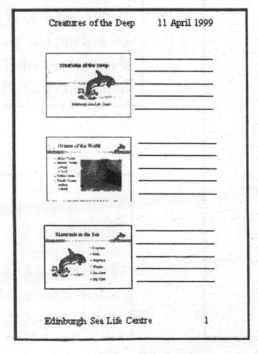

Handout printed 3 slides –
and notes – to a page

Printing notes pages

It is useful to print out your notes pages to help ensure you cover all the relevant points during your presentation. When these are printed, a copy of the slide is placed at the top of the page and your notes appear below it.

Printing the Outline

A printed outline can be very useful in that it lets you see an overview of the whole presentation. If you wish to print out a copy of the Outline view of your presentation, the same basic techniques are used. Your print will contain details of each slide title and the main points listed on each slide. Specify **Outline View** in the **Print what:** field to get the printout.

Creatures of the Deep   11 April 1999

Oceans of the World

Notes on the oceans of the world for PowerPoint presentation prepared for PowerPoint 2000 Made Simple.

I really don't know very much about the oceans of the world, but it seemed a good idea at the time.

Edinburgh Sea Life Centre   1

Take note

If you click the Print icon on the standard toolbar, one copy of each slide is printed. For anything else you must access the Print dialog box and select what you want to print in the Print what: field.

Take note

Page numbers are added automatically, unless you removed the number field from the Notes Master.

Basic steps

1 Display the slide you wish to preview.

❑ Grayscale preview

2 Click the Grayscale Preview tool ▨ on the Standard toolbar.

❑ Pure black and white preview

3 Hold the [Shift] key down and click ▨.

4 Click ▨ again to switch the Preview off.

❑ To change the printed appearance

5 Preview the slide in Grayscale or Pure black and white.

6 Right-click on the object.

7 Select Black and White from the pop-up menu.

8 Choose an option from the list.

Grayscale/black and white

The **Grayscale** and **Pure black and white** print options are useful for printing notes pages and handouts. The table below gives guidelines on how some of the objects print in **grayscale** and in **pure black and white**.

Object	Grayscale	Pure black and white
Text	Black	Black
Text shadows	Hidden	Hidden
Embossing	Hidden	Hidden
Fills	Grayscale	White
Frame	Black	Black
Pattern fills	Grayscale	White
Lines	Black	Black
Object shadows	Grayscale	Black
Slide backgrounds	White	White
Charts	Grayscale	Grayscale

● If you won't be printing your slides in colour, you can preview how a slide will look in **Grayscale** or **Pure black and white** on your screen.

● You can change the appearance of objects in **Grayscale** and **Pure black and white** if you wish.

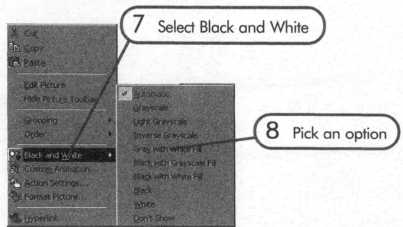

7 Select Black and White

8 Pick an option

133

Summary

❑ Specify your slide format before printing your presentation.

❑ It is often easier to specify your print range (if you don't want to print all of your slides) in Slide Sorter view.

❑ Handouts for your audiences can be printed with 2, 3, 4, 6 or 9 slides per page.

❑ Print the Notes page to act as prompts while you give your presentation.

❑ Take a print of Outline view if you want a summary of your complete presentation.

❑ Although most presentations are designed to be shown in colour, you can print in grayscale or black and white if you prefer.

12 Jumping and linking

Action Buttons

Action Buttons are found in the AutoShapes list on the Drawing toolbar. You can use the Action Buttons to jump from one place in your presentation to another, or to link you through to another presentation, file or program.

The Action Buttons can be added to any slide you wish – they become 'activated' when you are running your slide show.

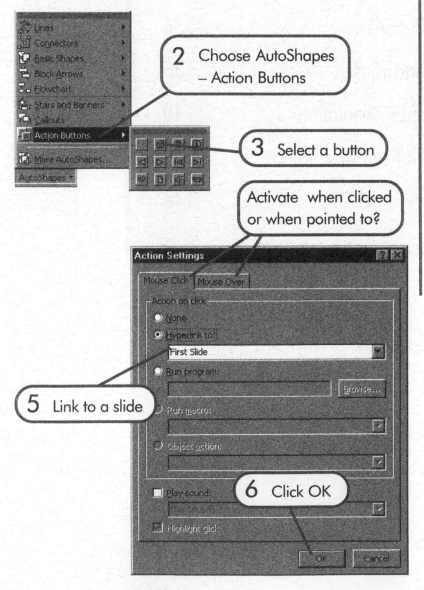

2 Choose AutoShapes – Action Buttons

3 Select a button

Activate when clicked or when pointed to?

5 Link to a slide

6 Click OK

1 Display the slide you want to put an Action Button on.

2 Choose Action Buttons from the AutoShapes menu.

3 Select a button.

4 Click on your slide to indicate where you want the button to appear.

5 At the Action Settings dialog box, select the slide to Hyperlink to.

6 Click ▓OK▓.

7 Resize or reposition the Action Button if necessary.

Tip

I suggest you go to Normal or Slide view for this section.

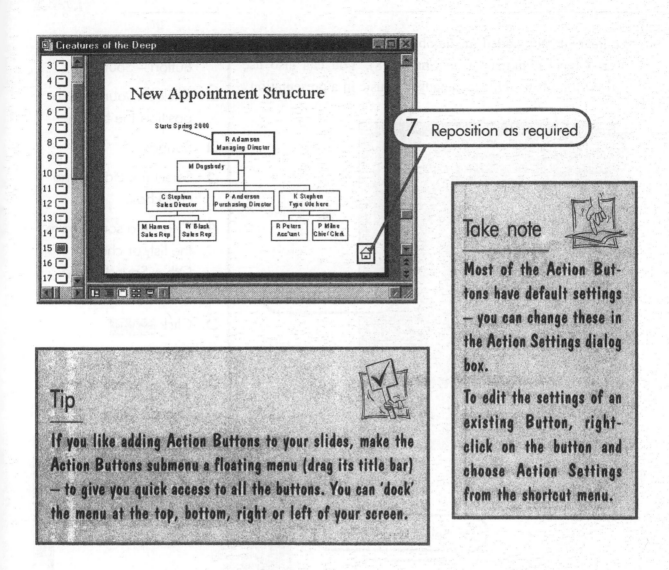

7 Reposition as required

Take note

Most of the Action Buttons have default settings — you can change these in the Action Settings dialog box.

To edit the settings of an existing Button, right-click on the button and choose Action Settings from the shortcut menu.

Tip

If you like adding Action Buttons to your slides, make the Action Buttons submenu a floating menu (drag its title bar) — to give you quick access to all the buttons. You can 'dock' the menu at the top, bottom, right or left of your screen.

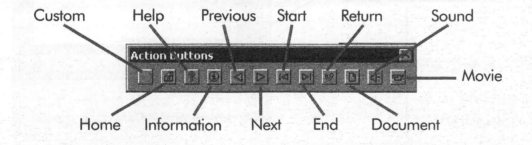

Custom   Help   Previous   Start   Return   Sound

Action Buttons

Movie

Home   Information   Next   End   Document

Sound and music

We have already added media objects to our slides using the Insert Object command (see Chapter 8). You can also use Action Buttons to activate sounds or music in a presentation.

1 Choose the Action Button – Sound .

2 Click on your slide to position the button.

❏ Sounds

3 Select the Play sound checkbox.

4 Choose a sound from the list, or choose Other Sound... and locate the sound file.

5 Click [OK].

❏ Music

6 Select Hyperlink to:

7 Choose Other File .

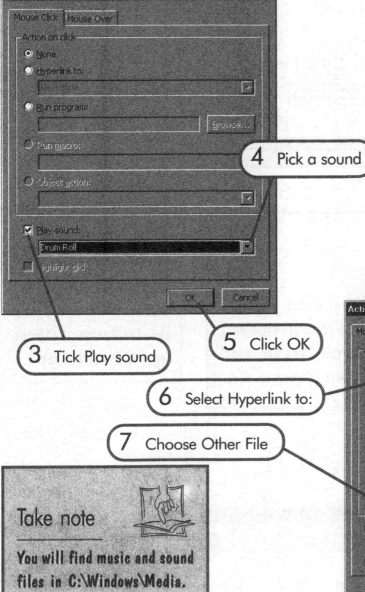

4 Pick a sound

3 Tick Play sound

5 Click OK

6 Select Hyperlink to:

7 Choose Other File

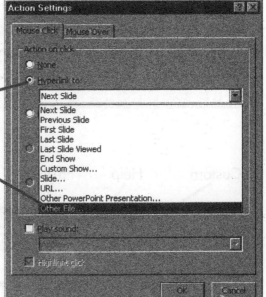

Take note

You will find music and sound files in C:\Windows\Media.

8 Locate your music file and click 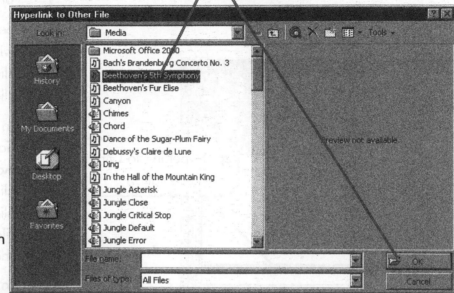 OK.

9 Click OK at the Action Settings dialog box.

8 Select the file and click OK

Actions can happen when you click the mouse, or pass the mouse over the button

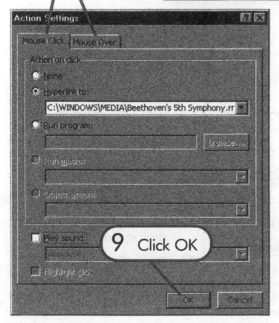

9 Click OK

When playing music, the Windows Media Player window appears so you can control the music. Minimise the window if you don't want it displayed.

Mixed slide orientation

In any PowerPoint file, the slide orientation is either landscape (the default) or portrait. You can't have some of the slides landscape and some portrait in the same file. If you want a presentation with some slides in one orientation and some in the other, Action Buttons and Hyperlinks can help out. You need to set up two files – one with the slide orientation landscape and the other portrait.

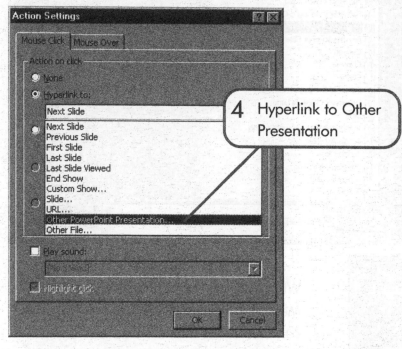

4 Hyperlink to Other Presentation

Take note

When you giving your presentation, click the Action Button to jump to the second file when you reach the appropriate slide. View the slides in the second file, moving between them as normal. To return to the main presentation file, press [Esc].

Basic steps

1 Set up your main presentation file – leaving out any slides that are in the other orientation.

2 Set up a second file with the remaining slides – with the other slide orientation set.

3 In the main presenta-tion file, place an Action Button on the slide that precedes a slide from the second file – I suggest you use the Custom button.

4 In Hyperlink to: choose Other PowerPoint Presentation.

5 Select the file that contains your slide(s) and click OK.

6 Specify the slide you want to jump to.

7 Click OK to close the Hyperlink to Slide dialog box.

8 Click OK to close the Action Settings dialog box.

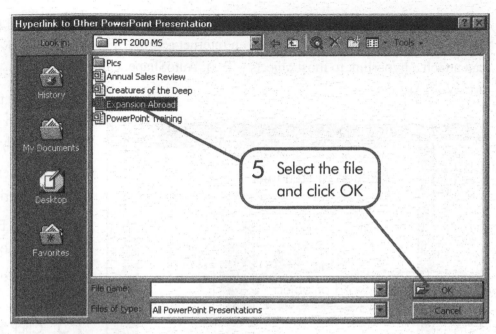

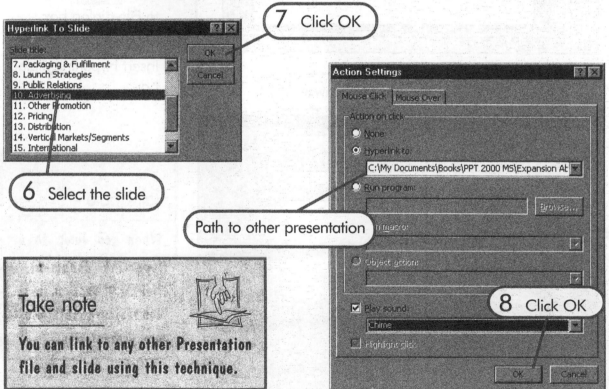

Hyperlink from any object

You don't have to use Action Buttons to hyperlink to different places in your file, to another file or to an Internet address. You can attach a hyperlink to most objects – Text, AutoShape, Clip art, WordArt, etc.

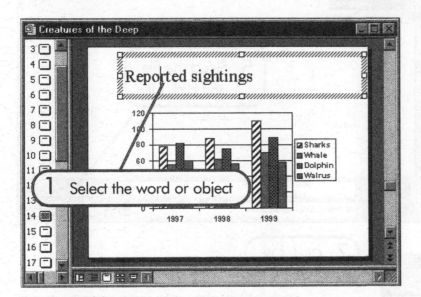

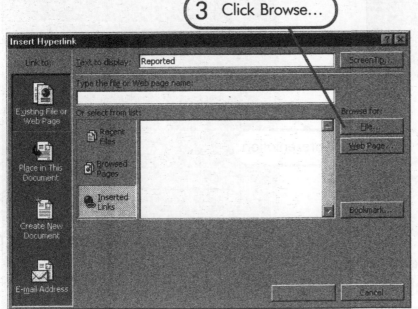

1 Select the object to hold the Hyperlink.

Or

Place the insertion point within the word to hold the Hyperlink.

2 Click the Insert Hyperlink tool ▨.

3 Click Browse… to look for the file.

4 Locate the folder and file.

5 Click ☐ ok ☐ at the Link to File dialog box.

6 Click ☐ ok ☐ at the Insert Hyperlink dialog box..

Take note

When you jump to a Hyperlink document, click ← Back on the Web toolbar to return to your presentation.

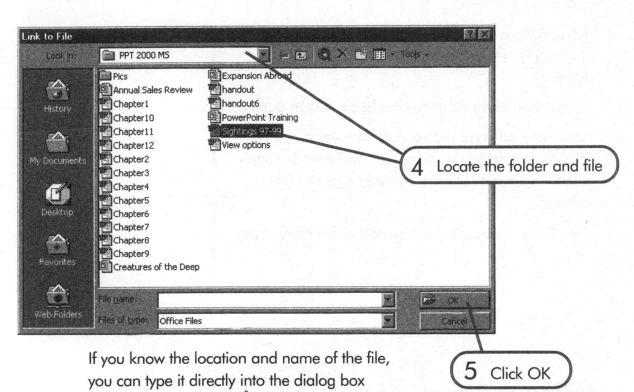

4 Locate the folder and file

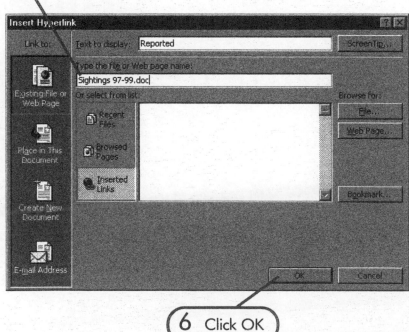

5 Click OK

If you know the location and name of the file, you can type it directly into the dialog box

Take note

During your slide show, you can 'jump' to the Hyperlink using your chosen method — either 'mouse click' or 'mouse over'.

6 Click OK

143

Summary

❑ Action Buttons provide a quick point and click method of jumping between slides, files and Internet addresses.

❑ Sounds and movies can be attached to Action Buttons.

❑ If you have different slide orientations within one presentation, create two separate files (one for each orientation) and insert hyperlinks between the two files as necessary.

❑ Hyperlinks can be attached to most of the object types on your slides.

Index